P9-DND-118

Donna
Merry Christmas
2002
Love
Mom + Dad

Gloria Copeland

Hidden Treasures:
Abundant Living
in the Riches of Proverbs

Hidden Treasures:
Abundant Living
in the Riches of Proverbs

By Gloria Copeland

Harrison House
Tulsa, Oklahoma

Unless otherwise indicated, all Scripture quotations are taken from the *King James Version* of the Bible.

Scripture quotations marked AMP are taken from *The Amplified Bible, Expanded Edition.* Copyright © 1987 by The Zondervan Corporation, Grand Rapids, Michigan, and The Lockman Foundation. All rights reserved. Used by permission.

Scripture quotations marked NIV are taken from the *Holy Bible: New International Version*® NIV®. Copyright © 1973, 1978, 1984 by the International Bible Society. Used by permission of Zondervan Publishing House. All rights reserved.

Direct quotations from the Bible appear in bold type.

Hidden Treasures:
Abundant Living in the Riches of Proverbs
ISBN 1-57794-129-2
Copyright © 1998 by Gloria Copeland
Kenneth Copeland Ministries
Fort Worth, Texas 76192-0001

Published by Harrison House, Inc.
P. O. Box 35035
Tulsa, Oklahoma 74153

Printed in the United States of America. All rights reserved under International Copyright Law. Contents and/or cover may not be reproduced in whole or in part in any form without the express written consent of the Publisher.

Dedication

I take pleasure in dedicating *Hidden Treasures* to the Partners of Kenneth Copeland Ministries.

Thank you for your willingness to obey God and stand with us so faithfully all these years. As Ken often says, "We have the most faithful Partners in the world!"

Because you have partnered with us, we have been able to minister the goodness of God and proclaim that Jesus is Lord and Savior around the world.

Together we are a voice — a Voice of Victory!

Your Partner,
Gloria Copeland

We love you. We care about you. We deeply appreciate you.

Contents

Acknowledgement

Special thanks to my sister Missy Johnson for her encouragement and assistance in the preparation of this book.

Introduction

God has a wonderful life planned for each one of us, but many live and die and never walk the path of His perfect will because they fail to find out enough about Him to cooperate with His plan.

Godly wisdom is comprehensive insight into the ways and purposes of God. **The Wisdom... of the prudent is to understand his way...** (Proverbs 14:8, AMP). The Word of God is the wisdom of God. As He spoke His will to men through the years, it has been written down and preserved. The Bible says God never changes. There is no shadow of turning with Him. He can't change. He's right!

His ways, when obeyed, work wonderful victory in this life, even overcoming the curse that came into the earth when Adam and Eve disobeyed God in the Garden of Eden. The curse of sin includes all the death, darkness, sickness, poverty, insecurity, fear and doubt that surround us.

God is a good God. He has always desired His family to live free, well and in the abundance of all good things. God gives us His wisdom so freely in His Word because He wants us to be able to live a victorious, overcoming life to His glory even while we are here in the earth.

In Proverbs, God gives us the riches of His principles, His wisdom and His direction that will cause us to live in His light in a dark world. He offers them to anyone who will listen. The book of Proverbs truly is a treasure to anyone who wants God's will in his life. We can read in black and white what, according to God, is the right (righteous) way for us in the situations, relationships and affairs of this life.

If we will obey His written wisdom that we can see and understand plainly, we will also be able to discern the paths of life that we are to individually walk. God's promises in Proverbs are so wonderful for those who will listen and do what He says. God says the result of following His ways is life, counsel, sound knowledge, understanding, might and power, health, length of days, His favor, peace, riches and honor.

God is saying to us, "This is the right thing to do. Here it is. I'm offering you My best. You can take Me and My ways if you desire — or you can reject My truth that will make you free." I don't know what you're going to do, but as for me and my house, we're going to listen and obey God's wisdom and live!

Come with me. Let's go treasure hunting. We get to keep all the treasure we find!

CHAPTER 1
The Beginning of Wisdom

You can only walk in the wisdom and blessings
of God as you learn to reverence and give Him honor
in your life.

Proverbs Chapter 1

1 The proverbs of Solomon the son of David, king of Israel;

2 To know wisdom and instruction; to perceive the words of understanding;

3 To receive the instruction of wisdom, justice, and judgment, and equity;

4 To give subtilty to the simple, to the young man knowledge and discretion.

5 A wise man will hear, and will increase learning; and a man of understanding shall attain unto wise counsels:

6 To understand a proverb, and the interpretation; the words of the wise, and their dark sayings.

7 The fear of the Lord is the beginning of knowledge: but fools despise wisdom and instruction.

8 My son, hear the instruction of thy father, and forsake not the law of thy mother:

9 For they shall be an ornament of grace unto thy head, and chains about thy neck.

10 My son, if sinners entice thee, consent thou not.

11 If they say, Come with us, let us lay wait for blood, let us lurk privily for the innocent without cause:

12 Let us swallow them up alive as the grave; and whole, as those that go down into the pit:

13 We shall find all precious substance, we shall fill our houses with spoil:

14 Cast in thy lot among us; let us all have one purse:

15 My son, walk not thou in the way with them; refrain thy foot from their path:

16 For their feet run to evil, and make haste to shed blood.

17 Surely in vain the net is spread in the sight of any bird.

18 And they lay wait for their own blood; they lurk privily for their own lives.

19 So are the ways of every one that is greedy of gain; which taketh away the life of the owners thereof.

20 Wisdom crieth without; she uttereth her voice in the streets:

21 She crieth in the chief place of concourse, in the openings of the gates: in the city she uttereth her words, saying,

22 How long, ye simple ones, will ye love simplicity? and the scorners delight in their scorning, and fools hate knowledge?

23 Turn you at my reproof: behold, I will pour out my spirit unto you, I will make known my words unto you.

24 Because I have called, and ye refused; I have stretched out my hand, and no man regarded;

25 But ye have set at nought all my counsel, and would none of my reproof:

26 I also will laugh at your calamity; I will mock when your fear cometh;

27 When your fear cometh as desolation, and your destruction cometh as a whirlwind; when distress and anguish cometh upon you.

28 Then shall they call upon me, but I will not answer; they shall seek me early, but they shall not find me:

29 For that they hated knowledge, and did not choose the fear of the Lord:

30 They would none of my counsel: they despised all my reproof.

31 Therefore shall they eat of the fruit of their own way, and be filled with their own devices.

32 For the turning away of the simple shall slay them, and the prosperity of fools shall destroy them.

33 But whoso hearkeneth unto me shall dwell safely, and shall be quiet from fear of evil.

Hidden Treasures

We don't have to go very far into the book of Proverbs before God tells us why He inspired Solomon to write it: **That people may know skillful and godly Wisdom and instruction, discern and comprehend the words of understanding and insight** (Proverbs 1:2, AMP).

To Instruct in Wisdom

Skillful and godly wisdom is actually the greatest blessing God could ever give us. The understanding and insight that come from God can help us live on this earth almost as if we were already in heaven!

People who choose God and His ways have a tremendous advantage in life. We can live and move in the kingdom of God today — right now — not just after we get to heaven. We are citizens of heaven (Philippians 3:20, NIV). We are to live in this earth in the blessing and power of God.

We are born of God with His very own Spirit living inside us, to teach and direct us. We no longer are just in the world. We have already been translated (at the new birth) out of the kingdom of darkness and into the kingdom of

His dear Son. We are living and operating in the kingdom of God now (Colossians 1:13). But we can only operate in God's kingdom by His wisdom — His way of doing and being right!

But if you don't tap into the wisdom of God that is available to you as a believer, you will continue to live much the same way you did before you were born again.

I can look back on my own life and see the truth of that statement. Ken and I were born again and filled with the Holy Spirit for five years before we ever experienced significant changes in our natural circumstances. That's because we hardly knew anything about God's Word.

We wanted to live for God, but we didn't know how. We didn't know God's ways so it was impossible for us to cooperate with Him to overcome our problems. But as soon as we began to learn more about His Word and apply it to our lives, our circumstances immediately began to change for the better.

Higher Life

The book of Proverbs gives us **instruction in wise dealing and the discipline of wise thoughtfulness, righteousness, justice, and integrity** (Proverbs 1:3, AMP). These words of wisdom are so plain and so easy to understand that even the simple can receive prudence and discretion (v. 4).

God made earth to be a copy of heaven (and ultimately He's going to get His way). The earth was created by the Word and the wisdom of God and it responds to the Word and wisdom of God. Adam was to manage the earth according to the same wisdom, thus allowing the Father to continually meet his every need. God wanted man to literally have days of heaven on earth.

Heaven looks so good to us because its atmosphere is full of the mercy, love, justice, righteousness and abundance in which we were created to live, not apart from God but with God. We were created to live in agreement with God and to do what is right in His sight because after all, He created us and He is our God. Imagine what it would be like to live in a world where there was no disobedience and the law of love was never broken. THAT WOULD BE HEAVEN!

You can learn how to live your life in a way that works without going through a lot of trial and error.

It's true that you can learn from your mistakes, but experience still isn't the best teacher. The best teacher is the Word of God. And, whether you're young or old, the best way to live your life is to learn God's wisdom so you can avoid pitfalls.

That prudence may be given to the simple, and knowledge, discretion, and discernment to the youth (v. 4, AMP).

Use Proverbs to teach your children to choose what is right. Start early and the wisdom of God will hold them steady all their lives. You don't have to wait until you are seventy-five years old to find out what works in life. God tells you what works! The truth is, many seventy-five-year-old people still don't know how to make their lives right.

The wise also will hear and increase in learning, and the person of understanding will acquire skill and attain to sound counsel [so that he may be able to steer his course rightly] (v. 5, AMP).

These proverbs are not only for the simple and the youth, but also for the wise to increase in learning. So whatever category we fit into — whether we're simple and naive, young and inexperienced or wise in our knowledge of God's ways — we can learn and grow through continually studying the book of Proverbs.

Walking in the Fear of God

Where do we start in our quest for godly wisdom? God tells us exactly where to begin: **The reverent and worshipful fear of the Lord is the beginning and the principal and choice part of knowledge [its starting point and its essence]; but fools despise skillful and godly Wisdom, instruction, and discipline** (Proverbs 1:7, AMP).

Walking in the fear of God is the beginning of wisdom. In fact, it's the only place there is to start! You will never be able to walk in the wisdom of God unless you reverence Him and give Him honor in your life. Without honoring God and giving Him His place of preeminence, you will continue to walk after your own desires instead of His and you'll never experience the high life of God's plan for your life.

The more you change your decisions and your lifestyle to line up with God's Word, the more honor you are giving God in your life. And God said, **For them that honour me I will honour** (1 Samuel 2:30).

Failure to honor God is when you face a choice between going God's way or your way and you choose to do what *you* want to do instead of what He says. A lack of reverence for God is what causes the foolish to **eat of the fruit of their own way** (Proverbs 1:31, AMP).

To eat the fruit of your own way is to experience the consequences of choosing to be your own god — and that's a pitiful situation in which to find yourself! When you exalt and obey your desires more than you exalt and obey God's desires for your life, you take yourself out of God's hands and separate yourself from His provision. You become your only deliverance — and we all know that relying on ourselves for deliverance just isn't enough!

For example, after Adam disobeyed God, he had to live by the sweat of his brow instead of according to the provision of God. His disobedience forced him to live under a curse that he could not cure. He ate the fruit of his own way.

But when you go God's way, you eat the fruit of *His* way, and His way is good. The abundant life He gives is full of love, joy, peace, goodness, kindness and all the fruit of the spirit listed in Galatians 5:22 and 23.

Give God first place over all your desires, over your own ambitions — over *everything* in your life. That kind of honor and reverence for God will pull you back from the snare of temptation to do wrong and cause you to do what's right. And as you walk in God's ways, your obedience will bring continual good in your life. His life is the "good life."

I remember when Ken and I first found out about the integrity of God's Word. We were so excited to learn that the Bible was just like God talking to us personally — that we could act on it, count on it and base our lives on it. So we made a decision that we would honor God by obeying His Word. Whatever we saw in the Word, we would do — whether we wanted to or not. And there were definitely times when we saw something we *didn't* want to do. But we did it anyway, because God had commanded us to do it. (By the way, when we fail at this we repent, receive forgiveness and start again!)

That kind of quality decision is necessary if you want a successful life in God. You must decide, "I'm going God's way, come hell or high water! I choose God's will for my life. Whether it seems easy or difficult, I'm going to do what the Word says."

A person who makes that type of decision cannot be defeated. Nothing can keep him from success. No devil in hell can keep him bound because commitment to God's way brings success. On the other hand, every single choice that goes against God's laws will only produce sin and death. The Scripture says that the wages of sin is death; but the gift of God is eternal life through Jesus Christ our Lord (Romans 6:23). So if you want to walk in God's kind of life, you have to walk in His ways.

For they that are after the flesh do mind the things of the flesh; but they that are after the Spirit the things of the Spirit. For to be carnally minded is death; but to be spiritually minded is life and peace (Romans 8:5-6).

If you choose to walk the world's way, you're going to have a hard walk. And in the end, you will come out defeated and worse off than you were before.

My son, hear the instruction of your father... (Proverbs 1:8, AMP). The key to life in the wisdom of God is "Hear!"

All through the Bible God has required of His people this one thing: "Hear what I say and do it!" As you read the Bible watch how many times God says to hear or hearken. How we hearken determines our outcome in every situation.

A revelation of hearing and obeying God is the Basic Bible Course to Victory!

When temptation and pressure come, the wisdom of God will cause you to choose God's way if you truly reverence Him as God.

The Lifestyle of the Wise

೫(˙^˙)ೂ

Greed **takes away the lives of its possessors** (Proverbs 1:19, AMP). That's why God tells you not to covet or lust after the things of this world. He knows that it ultimately takes away your life. On the other hand, obeying His Word brings peace and life and joy.

Now, it's all right to desire to increase financially and materially; it is even God's will for you to be blessed and to continually increase. But an intense desire for material gain at the expense of your walk with God is an entirely different thing.

Greed is just one of the sins that takes away the lives of those who yield to it. Even though you may enjoy some sins of the flesh for a season, sooner or later you will also have to endure the consequences of yielding to temptation — consequences that you *won't* enjoy.

The devil isn't going to do you any favors. He can't even bless his own people. The more faithfully a person serves Satan, the more of a death hold Satan has on that person. The devil just can't do you *any* good!

Proverbs 1:10-19 talks about resisting big temptations to sin, such as associating with ungodly people who would entice you to steal. Many times the Lord has corrected me about things that seem so small that many would not even think twice about them. But the more time we spend with God, the more sensitive we become to Him and the more successful we become in living a life of freedom.

You see, walking in the wisdom of God is a way of life — a lifestyle we must choose daily. And God doesn't want us to choose His ways only in the big, important situations of life. We have to learn to allow God to prick our spirit about the little things we do that are not pleasing to Him. I call it "fine-tuning." If we will learn to hear Him in the little things, it will be easy to hear Him in the big situations of life.

God may deal with you about something that no one else would think anything about. But if you want to grow in God, be quick to hear and change even the little things.

For instance, if you spoke too harshly to someone, face up to it. Be quick to erase the offense by asking the person's forgiveness. Call that person on the telephone and say, "I'm sorry I said that to you. I shouldn't have been so harsh. I shouldn't have gotten out of love." That's the way to be blessed and to walk in the wisdom of God!

Wisdom Isn't Holding Back

It is encouraging to know that **Wisdom *cries aloud* in the street, she raises her voice in the markets** (v. 20, AMP).

This scripture is letting us know that wisdom isn't holding back from us or staying hidden; she isn't making it hard for us to lay hold of her. Instead, she is *crying aloud* in the street. **She cries at the head of the noisy intersections [in the chief gathering places]; at the entrance of the city gates she speaks** (v. 21, AMP).

Wherever people gather, wisdom cries aloud, saying, "Go this way! Don't follow the way of sin."

Wisdom is also with you wherever you go, telling you, "Do this. Change that. Go this direction. Think this thought instead of that one." The Scripture tells us why wisdom can be our constant companion: **If any of you lack wisdom, let him ask of God, that *giveth to all men liberally*, and upbraideth not;**

and it shall be given him (James 1:5). God's great desire is for us to walk in wisdom. First Corinthians 1:30 says that **Christ Jesus...is made unto us wisdom.** Wisdom is something that already belongs to us. The Apostle Paul prayed for the church at Ephesus that God would give them the spirit of wisdom and revelation in the knowledge of Him, that the eyes of their understanding would be enlightened. We should pray this prayer for ourselves. God wants us to have wisdom (Ephesians 1:17-23).

Four Classes of People

God puts people in four different classes in relation to wisdom. Wisdom pleads with three of those classes of people.

First, there are *the simple* — those who are open to evil, ready to go any direction that someone might tell them to go.[1] Now, it *is* possible for the simple to go in the direction of the Word. If they do, God will give them wisdom and prudence so they won't be simple anymore. Instead, they'll begin to operate in discretion.

Then there are *the scoffers* or *scorners*. These are people who have been open to evil so long, they aren't simple any longer. They have pushed so long against God's wisdom, their hearts have ceased to be open to good. They won't even let others talk to them about God.

The further these scorners went in the way of evil, the more they became hardened to the voice of wisdom. Now their hearts are hardened and cold, and they mock everything that's right.

You see, if a person stays simple, sooner or later he will begin to do what is wrong. If he doesn't repent and begin to listen to wisdom, he eventually becomes a hardened scorner who mocks the things of God. As a scorner, he shuts himself off even more tightly from the wisdom of God.

And if that person continues in the way of the scorner, he will finally end up in the third class of people: those who are *fools*. A fool is even further down the path that leads away from God. His heart is even more hardened against God than the scorner. The fool is absolutely determined to set himself against God.

Finally, there is the fourth class of people: those who are *wise*. That's the class you want to be in. You don't want to stay simple. You don't want to be a

---

[1] James Strong, "Hebrew Dictionary of the Old Testament," *The New Strong's Exhaustive Concordance of the Bible* (Nashville: Thomas Nelson Publishers, 1995), p. 97, #6612.

scorner or a fool. You want to become wise. That's why wisdom cries aloud, endeavoring to tell each of us the wise thing to do. And if we will just stop and listen to what wisdom (or God) is saying, God promises to make His Word known to us. We will begin to understand how to walk in goodness, peace, justice and integrity.

Eating the Fruit of Their Own Ways

But what if the simple one goes on being simple? What if the scorner keeps on mocking and the fool stays hardened to what God is trying to tell him?

Proverbs 1:25-32 in *The Amplified Bible* gives a clear idea of what happens to those who treat as nothing all of wisdom's counsel: When their **panic comes as a storm and desolation** (v. 27), and they finally turn to wisdom for help, they'll find out that they have to **eat of the fruit of their own way and be satiated with their own devices** (v. 31). Although they seek wisdom early and diligently, they will not find her (v. 28).

You see, whether or not we eat the fruit of our own way is up to us. If we want to go God's way, then we'll eat His fruit of goodness, peace and instruction. But if we want to go the way of the world, we will ultimately eat its bitter fruit.

Sometimes a person dies young and people ask, "Why did God let this happen?" But God didn't just let it happen. Often a spiritual law has been set in motion that God can't change because God lives by His own Word. **...If we deny him, he also will deny us: If we believe not, yet he abideth faithful: he cannot deny himself** (2 Timothy 2:12-13).

For instance, perhaps that person wouldn't walk with God. Perhaps he was obstinate in his heart and wouldn't allow the wisdom of God to correct him to do what he knew was right.

If so, then a spiritual law *has* gone into effect: the law that says *sin brings death*.

Many Christians, even though they are born again, never go after God and His way of doing things. As a result, it is very easy for them to be beaten at the game of life. They don't practice hearing and obeying God, so they live pretty much like the world lives. Our part is to draw nigh to God. He shouldn't have to chase us down. Remember, we are to seek Him and His way of doing and being right.

There are consequences to living your life unregulated by God's Word. Even simply doing nothing when God speaks is enough to affect you adversely because doing nothing when God has spoken what to do is disobedience. And there's a price to pay when you disobey.

Just think about it. Sins of the flesh — drunkenness, tobacco, drugs, promiscuous sex, fits of anger, unforgiveness — not only take the spiritual life out of us if we yield to them, but they can also cause us to die young.

That's the way sin is. And that's why God tells us not to do it. He warns us that **the backsliding of the simple shall slay them, and the careless ease of [self-confident] fools shall destroy them** (Proverbs 1:32, AMP).

God Is True to His Word

If God says, "Do this, and you'll be blessed," then you can know you'll be blessed if you obey what He's told you to do. It doesn't matter what is happening in the world around you, you will be blessed because God remains true and faithful to His Word and His righteous character.

But what happens if God warns you, "The end of this way is death — don't do it," and you do it anyway? Sooner or later, you'll experience problems, trouble and sorrow. You can just count on it. God's admonition is true. He cannot lie.

For example, just look at the children of Israel. God told Israel through many, many supernatural events and messengers, "Do this, and you'll have good success. But if you disobey My commandments, other nations will conquer and enslave you. Terrible things will come upon you."

God was true to His Word. When Israel refused to listen to God's many warnings, they enabled the curse of the law to come upon them.

As Christians we have been redeemed from that curse by the blood of Jesus (Galatians 3:13). But if we continue to act, think and talk like the world, we will suffer the same consequences for sin that the world does.

Listen to Wisdom

Now is the time to get rid of any habit in your life that isn't pleasing to God. You don't ever have to yield to sin's temptation because sin has lost its dominion over you (Romans 6:14). That means the answer to temptation is, *Don't do it.* Turn it down. Don't consent.

You have a will of your own. When wisdom talks to you, jump up and listen! Make some changes. If God deals with an area of your life that you need to correct, be quick to change. The end of disobedience is death, but the end of walking with God is eternal life.

Do you see why it's so important to take time in the Word and in prayer? You need to tell God every day, "I put You first place in my life. I know if I follow You, everything else in my life will fall in place. Show me where I'm wrong. Correct me. Instruct me. Reveal to me the things I need to know." Then whatever He says to you, do it!

It's hard for you to hear while you're busy watching television. If you are distracted with other things all the time, you can't expect to hear God clearly on a regular basis. You have to give Him the opportunity to talk to you by setting aside time to get quiet, study His Word and pray.

Hearing from heaven is the most important thing in your entire life, because man has never faced a problem big enough to stump God. God always has an answer. He always has a way to bring you out of any trial victoriously, no matter how serious it is.

Don't let yourself be found among the simple, the scorners or the fools. Start at the beginning of wisdom — reverence God. Then watch your circumstances begin to change as you choose the lifestyle of the wise! The result is Proverbs 1:33 (AMP), **But whoso hearkens to me [Wisdom] shall dwell securely and in confident trust and shall be quiet, without fear or dread of evil.**

Wisdom for Today

Honor God in every choice or decision you make today.

Make the quality decision, "Whether it seems easy or difficult, I will do what the Word says."

Tell the Lord today, "Show me where I'm wrong. Reveal to me the things I need to know."

CHAPTER 2
Treasure God's Word

*Success in every area of life is ours to claim when we
treasure God's words and direct our hearts and minds
toward His wisdom.*

Proverbs Chapter 2

1   My son, if thou wilt receive my words, and hide my commandments with thee;

2   So that thou incline thine ear unto wisdom, and apply thine heart to understanding;

3   Yea, if thou criest after knowledge, and liftest up thy voice for understanding;

4   If thou seekest her as silver, and searchest for her as for hid treasures;

5   Then shalt thou understand the fear of the Lord, and find the knowledge of God.

6   For the Lord giveth wisdom: out of his mouth cometh knowledge and understanding.

7   He layeth up sound wisdom for the righteous: he is a buckler to them that walk uprightly.

8   He keepeth the paths of judgment, and preserveth the way of his saints.

9   Then shalt thou understand righteousness, and judgment, and equity; yea, every good path.

10 When wisdom entereth into thine heart, and knowledge is pleasant unto thy soul;

11 Discretion shall preserve thee, understanding shall keep thee:

12 To deliver thee from the way of the evil man, from the man that speaketh froward things;

13 Who leave the paths of uprightness, to walk in the ways of darkness;

14 Who rejoice to do evil, and delight in the frowardness of the wicked;

15 Whose ways are crooked, and they froward in their paths:

16 To deliver thee from the strange woman, even from the stranger which flattereth with her words;

17 Which forsaketh the guide of her youth, and forgetteth the covenant of her God.

18 For her house inclineth unto death, and her paths unto the dead.

19 None that go unto her return again, neither take they hold of the paths of life.

20 That thou mayest walk in the way of good men, and keep the paths of the righteous.

21 For the upright shall dwell in the land, and the perfect shall remain in it,

22 But the wicked shall be cut off from the earth, and the transgressors shall be rooted out of it.

Hidden Treasures

🙠

God gives us clear instructions for finding the hidden treasures in His Word: **My son, if you will** *receive* **my words and** *treasure up* **my commandments within you** (v. 1, AMP).

We should take this scripture as the Heavenly Father talking directly to us. The Father is telling us to *treasure* His words, making them the final authority in our lives.

Make Wisdom
the Quest of Your Life

🙠

In verse 2, more detail is given to explain what it means to treasure God's words: **Making your ear attentive to skillful and godly Wisdom and inclining and** *directing your heart and mind to understanding* **[applying all your powers to the quest for it]** (AMP).

This scripture agrees with James 1:5-6, which says when you want wisdom, you must ask for it in faith and not waver. Proverbs 2:2 takes that thought a step further and tells you to direct your mind and your heart toward God's wisdom.

You have to go after the wisdom and knowledge of God, applying all of your powers — your concentration, your energy, your efforts — to obtaining it. It has to become the quest of your life.

In fact, you must **search for skillful and godly Wisdom as for hidden treasures** (v. 4, AMP). The way to find wisdom is to go after it with the same effort and desire that natural people go after material wealth.

The truth is, no one ever seeks after God with all their heart without finding Him.

Suppose you seek after the knowledge and wisdom of God in a particular situation you're facing. You give God your time in prayer, and you find out what His Word has to say about it.

I'll tell you what happens when you make that kind of diligent effort — you **find the knowledge of God** (v. 5). When you obey what you find, you will begin to experience God's power working in that situation to bring you to victory.

You can be confident of that because **the Lord gives skillful and godly Wisdom; from His mouth come knowledge and understanding** (v. 6, AMP). You see, you'll never find anything coming from God's mouth except truth. Wisdom is truth and Jesus said that knowing the truth is what makes you free (John 8:32).

God has given us His wisdom in the written Word through Moses, through David, through Paul — through all the men who wrote the books of the Old and New Covenants. That divine wisdom is written down now in one Book, the Bible, so any time we want to we can receive the wisdom and knowledge we need for every situation.

We don't have to go through the experiences Moses went through to learn the lessons he learned. We can find out from the Word what God taught him.

Just think about what God has done for us! We have God's wisdom available to us in the written Word. We also have the Holy Spirit living inside us to teach and reveal this wisdom to us.

Moses couldn't do that. He didn't have the written Word. Even though Moses was inspired by the Holy Spirit when he wrote some of the Bible, he didn't have the entire written text to read whenever he desired as we do.

And the Apostle Paul didn't have the New Testament to read either. He had to go before God and receive revelation about the mystery of the gospel and then write down that revelation in letters to the churches.

But you and I do have the entire written Word. We have access to all the revelation written down in black and white that the men of the Bible received from God. Not only that, but we also have the Holy Spirit alive and working in us to give us revelation for today. Considering all the advantages that come with living in this day, we should be *far* ahead of where the early Church was spiritually!

God Stores Away Wisdom for Us

Of course, not just everyone can find God's wisdom. Only those who are ready for it, who desire and seek after God with all their heart, are willing to understand and receive His wisdom. That's because **He *hides away* sound and**

godly Wisdom and *stores* it for the righteous (those who are upright and in right standing with Him) (Proverbs 2:7, AMP).

God is always ready to be found, and His wisdom is always available. But those who don't seek Him don't find Him. The wisdom of God is hidden away, to be discovered only by those who serve Him, desire Him and give Him authority in their lives.

You see, God isn't hiding His wisdom *from* us; He's hiding wisdom *for* us.

Natural men just can't get hold of the wisdom of God. Now, some do discover certain elementary principles of God's wisdom that can bring a measure of success on this earth. They find out that the laws of God *are* the laws of success. So they write "how-to-be-a-success" books telling you to be honest and just. They tell you if you want a successful business, you need to maintain an attitude of serving others.

Many people have become millionaires by studying and applying the principles in these success books. They have used God's elementary principles to lay hold of material wealth.

But that's as far as natural man can go. If those same people aren't cleansed by the blood of Jesus and if all of God's wisdom isn't the quest of their lives, they can't lay hold of peace. They can't lay hold of divine healing. They can't lay hold of deliverance from every yoke of bondage.

But all of these blessings and more belong to us as God's children when we treasure God's words and direct our hearts and minds toward His wisdom. Not only can we have success in business and in our finances — we can have success in *every* area of life.

God's ways are ways of financial prosperity. But His ways are also ways of divine health and peace, and these blessings can't be obtained just by the elementary laws of the universe. You must dig into the Word and lay hold of the spiritual authority that brings healing, deliverance, prosperity and peace into your life.

Look at what Jesus told His disciples: **Unto you it is given to know the mystery of the kingdom of God: but unto them that are without** [the kingdom of God], **all these things are done in parables** (Mark 4:11). That's why Jesus explained the parables He used to His own followers: so they could live and walk in God's way.

Yes, natural man might discover some elementary principles of God's wisdom. But God hides the depths of His wisdom for the righteous — for those who search for His knowledge and understanding as for hidden treasures. God sees to it that His wisdom cannot be misused. It is too powerful.

God's Wisdom Is a Shield to Us

Here's another good reason to treasure God's Word: **He is a shield to those who walk uprightly and in integrity** (Proverbs 2:7, AMP).

God's way works. His ways of wisdom — the principles of His kingdom and of His Spirit — cause a shield to rise up before you protecting you from the devils, dangers, turmoil and stress that are here on this earth. That's why walking in God's wisdom makes life worth living.

The Bible promises us that God knows how to deliver the righteous. No matter what kind of danger, financial disaster or natural calamity threatens a nation, God knows how to deliver those who walk in obedience to Him. The Bible says **He preserves the way of His saints** (v. 8, AMP).

However, when God's children don't walk in obedience to Him, they hinder Him from protecting them. How? By rebelling against His principles and laws of wisdom.

You have to stay in agreement with Him. He won't change from His way in order to agree with you, even though He loves you. He can't change because He's right!

God is a shield to you when you move *with* Him instead of *against* Him. He can't be a shield to you when you live your life in opposition to Him. You have to walk in His ways.

And you can't do that in ignorance. You don't just automatically walk in the knowledge of God the moment you are born again. You must take time in the Word to find out what God says about the various situations of life. Eventually you learn to look at your actions and reactions to situations through God's eyes. You learn to think His higher thoughts and walk in His higher ways (Isaiah 55:9).

You see, when God's Word goes into our hearts and our minds, it allows us to think His higher thoughts. Those higher thoughts and higher ways are God's wisdom and knowledge working in us, delivering us from sickness, disease, depression and every other evil work for which the natural world has no answer. We're able to live a much higher way of life than natural people can live.

Discretion Will Watch Over You

When you put yourself in a position to move with God instead of against Him, eventually **you will understand righteousness, justice, and fair dealing [in every area and relation]; yes, you will understand every good path** (v. 9, AMP).

And how are you able to understand every good path? Because **skillful and godly Wisdom shall enter into your heart** (v. 10, AMP). You see, wisdom is not a matter of the head; it's a matter of the heart or the spirit. That's why when you walk in God's wisdom, His promise of discretion becomes a reality in your life: **Discretion shall watch over you, understanding shall keep you** (v. 11, AMP).

Discretion is the divine direction that rises up from your spirit as you are about to do what you shouldn't do. You may not necessarily be ready to commit sin, but you may be about to make a wrong turn in life, such as putting your children in the wrong school, accepting the wrong job, etc. When that happens, discretion will rise up in you and say, "Don't go this way. Go that way instead."

So make discretion your friend. Be quick to hear that divine instruction. It may just be a simple, little thing. For instance, you might be driving somewhere, and the Lord may tell you, "Don't go that route; go around the other way." And as you obey that inner nudge, you might just avoid an accident!

You can apply that same principle of discretion to your entire life. If you begin to go in a direction that leads you away from God's will for your life, discretion will rise up and say, "That isn't the right way; change direction and go this way."

Another good reason discretion watches over you is **to deliver you from the way of evil and the evil men** (v. 12, AMP). You see, discretion resides within your spirit. And as you walk in God's wisdom, discretion will rise up to deliver you from the evil way — from any trial, temptation or obstacle that Satan may have prepared for you.

The best time to resist temptation and avoid making a mistake is at the beginning when it first confronts you. So when you walk in the discretion and wisdom of God, He'll tell you what to do before you ever get into trouble.

This discretion can only watch over you as you live your life expecting to hear from heaven and are willing to obey what you hear. You have to pay attention to that new man on the inside — the one that God dwells in. You hear God in your heart. That is where He gives you direction. You can't get up in the morning planning to live your day by your own wits and still enjoy the protection of supernatural discretion! Remind your heart and mind every day, "God is the One Who leads me. I'm going to listen for His voice, and I'm going to hear from Him today."

God rarely ever comes in spectacular ways to guide you. Usually He just quietly rises up within you to show you the right way to go. So if you aren't expecting to hear from Him, you'll miss Him in the little things. And it's obeying God in little things that teaches you how to flow with Him in the big issues of life.

Always conduct yourself with the attitude, "The Holy Spirit is in me. I expect to hear from Him today. I expect Him to tell me how to do my job. I expect to hear from Him even in the little matters of life."

For instance, if you need to purchase an item, why go to fourteen stores looking for the right item at the best price? Hear from heaven and find out the right store the first time!

"Gloria, do you really think God cares about such trivial matters?" Yes, I believe God cares about everything *you* care about. And I believe the Holy Spirit dwells in you and the angels garrison round about you to minister to you all the time. God wants to make this life better for you. He wants to lead you in the affairs of life. He wants to take out the guesswork so you don't flounder through life, wondering what to do.

Discretion not only delivers you from temptations and mistakes, but it also delivers you from "the evil man" or the person who could harm you. Evil men are defined as those **who forsake the paths of uprightness to walk in the ways of darkness, who rejoice to do evil and delight in the perverseness of evil** (Proverbs 2:13-14, AMP).

When you walk in discretion and understanding, you won't be brought into bondage to that type of person. Discretion will rise up and say, "Don't follow him. Go the way of wisdom instead." Then you can make the decision to **walk in the way of good men, and keep to the paths of the [consistently] righteous (the upright, in right standing with God)** (v. 20, AMP).

Remember, when you walk in God's ways of wisdom and discretion, He causes a shield to rise up before you to protect you from the enemy's attacks. That shield of protection is the reward of the upright, whom God promises **shall dwell [securely] in the land, and the men of integrity, blameless and complete [in God's sight], shall remain in it** (v. 21, AMP).

Great rewards are in store for those who treasure God's words, and great dangers await for those who do not. So make sure that *you* are one of God's "treasure hunters"!

Wisdom for Today

Direct your heart and mind toward God's wisdom and knowledge.

Expect to hear from God today; don't miss Him in the little things.

Walk in discretion. Resist temptation as soon as it confronts you.

CHAPTER 3
The Blessings of Walking in God's Wisdom

Why should obtaining God's wisdom and knowledge become our quest in life? Because every blessing we ever receive to make our lives worth living has its source in the wisdom of God.

※

Proverbs Chapter 3

1   My son, forget not my law; but let thine heart keep my commandments:

2   For length of days, and long life, and peace, shall they add to thee.

3   Let not mercy and truth forsake thee: bind them about thy neck; write them upon the table of thine heart:

4   So shalt thou find favour and good understanding in the sight of God and man.

5   Trust in the Lord with all thine heart; and lean not unto thine own understanding.

6   In all thy ways acknowledge him, and he shall direct thy paths.

7   Be not wise in thine own eyes: fear the Lord, and depart from evil.

8   It shall be health to thy navel, and marrow to thy bones.

9   Honour the Lord with thy substance, and with the firstfruits of all thine increase:

10   So shall thy barns be filled with plenty, and thy presses shall burst out with new wine.

11   My son, despise not the chastening of the Lord; neither be weary of his correction:

12   For whom the Lord loveth he correcteth; even as a father the son in whom he delighteth.

13   Happy is the man that findeth wisdom, and the man that getteth understanding.

14   For the merchandise of it is better than the merchandise of silver, and the gain thereof than fine gold.

15   She is more precious than rubies: and all the things thou canst desire are not to be compared unto her.

16   Length of days is in her right hand; and in her left hand riches and honour.

17   Her ways are ways of pleasantness, and all her paths are peace.

18   She is a tree of life to them that lay hold upon her: and happy is every one that retaineth her.

19   The Lord by wisdom hath founded the earth; by understanding hath he established the heavens.

20   By his knowledge the depths are broken up, and the clouds drop down the dew.

21   My son, let not them depart from thine eyes: keep sound wisdom and discretion:

22   So shall they be life unto thy soul, and grace to thy neck.

23 Then shalt thou walk in thy way safely, and thy foot shall not stumble.

24 When thou liest down, thou shalt not be afraid: yea, thou shalt lie down, and thy sleep shall be sweet.

25 Be not afraid of sudden fear, neither of the desolation of the wicked, when it cometh.

26 For the Lord shall be thy confidence, and shall keep thy foot from being taken.

27 Withhold not good from them to whom it is due, when it is in the power of thine hand to do it.

28 Say not unto thy neighbour, Go, and come again, and to morrow I will give; when thou hast it by thee.

29 Devise not evil against thy neighbour, seeing he dwelleth securely by thee.

30 Strive not with a man without cause, if he have done thee no harm.

31 Envy thou not the oppressor, and choose none of his ways.

32 For the froward is abomination to the Lord: but his secret is with the righteous.

33 The curse of the Lord is in the house of the wicked: but he blesseth the habitation of the just.

34 Surely he scorneth the scorners: but he giveth grace unto the lowly.

35 The wise shall inherit glory: but shame shall be the promotion of fools.

Hidden Treasures

Proverbs 3 tells us some of the blessings we receive from walking in God's ways and keeping His words. It starts out by saying, **My son, forget not my law or teaching, but** *let your heart keep my commandments* (v. 1, AMP).

You see, it's only when you keep God's commandments from your heart that life becomes secure from the temptations of the enemy. Even the fact that you are born again doesn't give you total security against deliberately yielding to Satan's temptations. Security in this life only comes when your heart begins to keep God's Word.

A temptation is a solicitation to evil. When your heart keeps God's Word, you won't even allow yourself to think about committing adultery or some other sin just to suit yourself. You won't even consider displeasing God just for a moment's pleasure. Your honor and reverence for God and His Word is your protection against the devil's temptations. God's commandment becomes your shield.

A Long Life Worth Living

One of the benefits you can expect from letting your heart keep God's commandments is *long life*: **Length of days and years of a life [worth living] and tranquility [inward and outward and continuing through old age till death], these shall they add to you** (v. 2, AMP).

The wisdom of God will add length of days to you — and many years of a life worth living!

Walking with God and abiding in His Word causes you to live a long life. But not only will you receive length of days, those long days will also be full of the good things of God! God **satisfieth thy mouth with good things; so that thy youth is renewed like the eagle's** (Psalm 103:5).

Kenneth has confessed that scripture every day for years. You, too, ought to start believing God for your youth to be renewed when you're still in the prime of your life.

Even if you're older now, you can still believe God to keep you intact, undamaged and complete all the days of your life (1 Thessalonians 5:23). Learn to live in the supernatural power and anointing that resides on the inside of you. Give the Spirit of God words of faith that He can use to quicken your mortal flesh.

A woman once wrote us a letter, saying, "If I keep getting healed, how am I ever going to die?" But you don't have to be sick to die! All you have to do is leave your earthly tabernacle. When Moses left this earth, the Bible says his natural strength was not abated, and his eye was not dim (Deuteronomy 34:7).

It does me good to read about men and women of God who lived out the full number of their days without sickness or disease. When these godly saints were ready to depart from this world, they just peacefully left their mortal bodies behind and went to a far better place.

One great minister who had lived a long, fruitful life for God told his loved ones ahead of time, "I'm going to leave today at ten o'clock." The chariot of God was coming for him, and he knew exactly what time it would arrive! And at ten o'clock, the elderly minister just sat down in his easy chair in the presence of his family and quietly went home to be with the Lord.

You can believe for that kind of homegoing for yourself — *after* you have enjoyed length of days and are fully satisfied with a life that was worth living!

So don't start dying — start *living*. Walk in God's ways and His wisdom all the days of your life!

Supernatural Favor With God and Man

Let's look at another of God's hidden treasures — a nugget of His wisdom to help us live in His blessings: **Let not mercy and kindness [shutting out all hatred and selfishness] and truth [shutting out all deliberate hypocrisy or falsehood] forsake you; bind them about your neck, write them upon the tablet of your heart** (Proverbs 3:3, AMP).

In order to enjoy a good life and to live days worth living, you must determine to walk in the mercy and lovingkindness of God.

Showing lovingkindness to others is the very essence of walking in God's wisdom. That's how God operates. He walks in mercy and lovingkindness. He's quick to forgive, quick to bless, quick to help.

So let God be your example. Walk as He walks. Make lovingkindness and truth so much a part of your life that these godly qualities just seem to hang around your neck because they are always with you. You never leave them at home; you never forsake them. You write them on the tablet of your heart.

When lovingkindness and truth are that much a part of your life, God promises you supernatural favor: **So shall you find favor, good understanding, and high esteem in the sight [or judgment] of God and man** (Proverbs 3:4, AMP).

Walking in God's wisdom will not only make God think highly of you — it will make man think highly of you as well!

Now, someone may say, "But people don't treat me right. They don't relate to me. They ignore me and give me the cold shoulder." But do you know what the problem usually is with someone who says that? He hasn't bound mercy and kindness about his own neck!

Most of the time people who feel mistreated are actually mistreating others themselves. I know that because if a person walks in love, he is going to be loved back. There just isn't any question about it. Whatever a man sows, that's what he will also reap (Galatians 6:7).

People are hungry for love. They can't find someone to love them on every street corner — particularly if they aren't too lovely themselves! So when they find someone who loves them and is kind to them, they will usually return love and kindness to that person as well.

Mercy and lovingkindness are definitely part of God's wisdom to help you walk successfully in this life. When you walk in love and truth toward others, they will show you kindness and favor in return. You will also find favor with God. God's wisdom gives you favor and causes you to be promoted in every area of your life. That's God's promise to you! (Proverbs 4:8).

Direction for Life's Pathways

Supernatural guidance is another benefit you can expect as you **lean on, trust in, and be confident in the Lord with all your heart and mind and do not rely on your own insight or understanding** (Proverbs 3:5, AMP).

It's so important to listen to the Lord. Sometimes God will tell you to do something that isn't what you would have chosen if you had figured things out on your own. God does that because He's smarter than you are. He knows the end from the beginning (Isaiah 46:10). He knows far more than you and can give you divine insight into any situation.

If you lean on your own understanding, you'll be in trouble. You don't know enough to avoid failure. But when you **in all your ways know, recognize, and acknowledge Him** (Proverbs 3:6, AMP), God rises up within you with His wisdom and gives you the direction to victory.

So when you get up in the morning, acknowledge God. Tell Him, "I'm going to listen to You today, Father. I expect to hear from You. I don't know the answer to what faces me today, but I belong to You, and *You* know the answer. I'm leaning on You, Father. I acknowledge You in all my ways."

As you acknowledge God in all your ways, God *will* do what He has promised to do: **He will direct and make straight and plain your paths** (v. 6, AMP).

Health to Your Body

What makes your body healthy? Here are at least three clues: **Be not wise in your own eyes; reverently fear and worship the Lord and turn [entirely] away from evil** (Proverbs 3:7, AMP).

You can't be wise in your own eyes and be wise in God at the same time. In other words, as you begin to walk in God's wisdom, you begin to increase. God's blessings start coming your way. When that happens, remember Who caused you to prosper in the first place. Don't become a legend in your own mind, thinking you are somebody big and important.

Instead, fear and worship the Lord. Honor Him with your life. Turn entirely away from evil, and don't be wise in your own eyes. Be quick to walk in what is right in God's sight. Follow these ways of God's wisdom, and you will bring **health to your nerves and sinews, and marrow and moistening to your bones** (Proverbs 3:8, AMP).

Your Storage Places Filled With Plenty

We've talked about the importance of walking in the fear of God and giving honor to Him in every area of life. This is also certainly true in the financial realm. We can honor God with our money: **Honor the Lord with your capital and sufficiency [from righteous labors] and with the firstfruits of all your income** (Proverbs 3:9, AMP).

If you want God involved in your finances, you'll have to be a tither, giving the first 10 percent of your increase to the Lord. You have to honor God in your life not just with your words, but also with your actions and with your money.

Ken and I never made any progress financially until we started tithing. We only began to increase after we made a quality decision to tithe, whether or not we ate or paid our bills. We made the wise decision not to be a "God robber" (Malachi 3:8).

We had begun to tithe earlier, but we didn't last very long at it. We decided that we needed the money more than God did. So we fell by the wayside, going deeper and deeper in debt.

But five years after we were born again, we began to learn the Word of God concerning the tithe. We made the decision to tithe faithfully. Everything is easier if you know something about what you're doing! When we began to honor God in our finances, He began to help us increase financially.

God does know how to prosper. He really lives well. If you'll listen to Him financially, He will give you His wisdom concerning prosperity. He believes in prosperity. The Bible is full of teaching on God's will for increase.

You see, you must make sure you are honoring God in whatever area of life that you need help from Him. For instance, if it's healing you need, honor Him in the area of healing. Find scriptures that promise healing, and plant them firmly in your heart. Meditate on His Word. Believe it. Say it. When you do, you honor God.

And if it's money that you need, honor God in your finances by faithfully tithing and giving. Be sure that prosperity words from God are abiding in your heart in abundance. How will you know? When they are there in abundance they will talk to you and you'll talk them out your mouth (Matthew 12:34-35).

It's very important to your well-being that you tithe. I am convinced that tithing is the very foundation of financial prosperity.

You may say, "Well, I just can't afford to tithe." But you can't afford *not* to! If you don't make a quality decision to honor God with your money, this time next year you'll still be in the same — or worse! — financial position than you're in today.

But as you honor God with the 10 percent that belongs to Him, He'll get involved with the rest. The other 90 percent will go further than ever before because you have gotten the supernatural power of God involved with your finances. You have invited Him into your financial life.

Besides giving the Lord the firstfruits of your income, you are to honor Him **with your capital and sufficiency** (Proverbs 3:9, AMP). That's talking about giving into God's kingdom out of the financial resources you already have.

Let's say you have been a tither. You have given God the firstfruits of your income. Now your capital is building up. So what's next? Give and spend according to what honors God. You honor Him with what you have — not just with your tithes, but with your capital and sufficiency.

That's what you do if you want to increase, because it's only after you honor God with your money that the following promise goes into effect: **So shall your storage places be filled with plenty, and your vats shall be overflowing with new wine** (Proverbs 3:10, AMP).

Your "storage place" is probably your bank account. But whatever you consider as your storage place, God says it will be filled with plenty! The Word says "storage places" so expect big!

It's very important to have plenty in this life — plenty to feed your family, plenty to pay your bills and plenty for the work of God. It's difficult to live in peace when you can't buy groceries.

God understands that, so He has planned for His people to prosper. He wants them to not only have enough for themselves, but enough to help other people too. For instance, He planned for Israel to be so financially blessed that they could loan money to other nations (Deuteronomy 28:12).

God knows what you need. He wants you to have more than enough to meet those needs with plenty left over to help others. But if you don't honor Him first with your money, He isn't going to get involved in your finances.

So if you want to increase in the financial realm, learn to be faithful in tithing. Do it first — *absolutely* first. If you have to go without food in order to give God His part, go without food.

Of course, you have never seen the righteous forsaken or his seed begging bread. Tithing is the way to never go without. Instead, you'll watch your storage places fill up with plenty until they overflow with good things!

Chastening for Your Good

The Lord's chastening is another blessing we will receive as we walk in His ways: **My son, do not despise or shrink from** *the chastening of the Lord...***neither be weary of or impatient about or loathe or abhor His reproof** (Proverbs 3:11, AMP).

The truth is, God's reproof to us is one of the greatest blessings He ever gives us. It lets us know, "You're getting off My path in this area. Get back on track. Correct this. Let go of that. Do this. Don't do that." That kind of loving reproof is one of the greatest things God does for us to keep us walking in His ways.

In *Young's Analytical Concordance*, the word "chastening" is defined as *instruction* or *training*.[1] In *W. E. Vine's Expository Dictionary* it brings in *discipline* or *correction*.[2] So how does God instruct, educate and discipline us?

Well, He *doesn't* discipline or chasten us by giving us cancer. He disciplines us in our spirit by His Word. The Bible says that **[our earthly fathers] disciplined us for only a short period of time and chastised us as seemed proper and good to them; but He disciplines us** [in our spirits] **for our certain good, that we may become sharers in His own holiness** (Hebrews 12:10, AMP).

This book is in itself a chastening and a correction from God's Word. As you accept this teaching and let it correct any area in your life that isn't in line with the Word, you'll be chastened of the Lord. But it won't be unpleasant — it will be for your certain good!

---

[1] Robert Young, *Young's Analytical Concordance to the Bible* (Grand Rapids: William B. Eerdman's Publishing Co., 1970), p. 156.
[2] W. E. Vine, *Vine's Expository Dictionary of New Testament Words* (McLean, VA: MacDonald Publishing Co., n.d.), p. 185.

So, for instance, when the Word of God tells you to tithe, don't despise that word when you hear it. Be glad that God is chastening you, telling you, "This is what has been wrong with your finances. You've been robbing Me!" Be quick to be corrected and quick to change, realizing that **whom the Lord loves He corrects, even as a father corrects the son in whom he delights** (Proverbs 3:12, AMP).

Riches and Honor

God's wisdom is more important to attain than riches: **the gaining of it is better than the gaining of silver, and the profit of it better than fine gold** (Proverbs 3:14, AMP).

You see, when you gain wisdom, you can obtain not only healing, peace and other blessings of God, but gold and silver as well. God's wisdom will show you how to operate wisely in the affairs of life so you can prosper and have plenty.

On the other hand, if you just have silver and gold without God's wisdom, you won't know how to experience supernatural healing or peace. Besides, your lack of health and peace will prevent you from enjoying all your silver and gold!

God's wisdom is the only way you can have it all. That's why **skillful and godly Wisdom is more precious than rubies; and nothing you can wish for is to be compared to her** (Proverbs 3:15, AMP). When you realize the truth of that scripture, you will pursue God's wisdom and knowledge with everything that is in you.

In Proverbs 2 we found out that you obtain God's wisdom when you make it the quest of your life. You must desire it, ask for it, go after it. You can't waver.

When you go after God's wisdom, you'll find out that **length of days is in her right hand, and in her left hand are riches and honor** (Proverbs 3:16, AMP).

That's a good scripture to get hold of if you've been wanting to know for sure whether or not it is God's will to prosper you. But understand that if you change your focus and go after riches and honor instead of wisdom, you probably won't live long enough to enjoy them even if you find a way to get them!

When you seek first God and His righteousness, wisdom brings you into all the blessings of God. However, wisdom teaches you to keep those blessings in the right priority.

Riches and honor in the wrong priority bring death. So if you want things to work right in your life, always keep your priorities in the proper order — with God and His wisdom at the top of your list!

A Life of Pleasantness and Peace

When we walk in God's wisdom, our paths in life are peaceful: **Her** [wisdom's] **ways are highways of pleasantness, and all her paths are peace. She is a tree of life to those who lay hold on her; and happy (blessed, fortunate, to be envied) is everyone who holds her fast** (Proverbs 3:17-18, AMP).

Now, that's the way we want to live: in pleasantness and peace! *The Companion Bible* says that *peace* in Hebrew means *well-being* or *prosperity.* Wisdom is a tree of life. God's blessings come as we hold fast to His wisdom (v. 18). Through the wisdom of God we can have a tree of life and live in God's Garden again!

Now let's see *why* wisdom works so proficiently in this natural realm: **The Lord by skillful and godly Wisdom has founded the earth; by understanding He has established the heavens** (Proverbs 3:19, AMP).

Everything in earth and in heaven was created to respond to God's wisdom. That's why wisdom works to drive back the enemy's works of darkness, such as sickness, disease, poverty and oppression.

You see, this earth was *created* by the wisdom of God, so it obeys the wisdom of God. And when we walk in God's wisdom and live according to His ways, evil is defeated. God's wisdom and understanding make life work right even in the midst of a dark, dangerous world full of stress and turmoil. The Light of God overcomes all the darkness.

On the other hand, this earth was *not* created to respond to the laws of sin and death. It rebels against those renegade laws that the enemy introduced into this natural realm with the fall of man. When we operate contrary to God's wisdom, heaven and earth are hindered from responding on our behalf. God's enemy is given place to operate *against* us because we are living according to the laws of sin and death.

You can't live ruled by sin and death and arrive at any kind of good destination on this earth. Sin and death aren't going anywhere good.

But you *can* choose to live in wisdom, honoring God and walking in truth, mercy and lovingkindness. When you walk in wisdom, your life just purrs right along on the highways of pleasantness and the pathways of peace. And you'll be able to walk securely and in confident trust through a very insecure world, **for the Lord shall be your confidence, firm and strong, and shall keep your foot from being caught [in a trap or some hidden danger]** (v. 26, AMP).

I guarantee you, when danger, trials or bad situations come your way, you'll be so glad that you have been walking in the wisdom of God. You'll be so glad you can go before the throne of God with great confidence to receive grace and help in time of need (Hebrews 4:16), because you have been doing the will of God.

God's Blessings and Grace
Upon Your Home

ᗍᙅ

Proverbs 3:31-35 contrasts the consequences of living by the law of sin and death or the wisdom of God. For instance, we are warned, **Do not resentfully envy and be jealous of an unscrupulous, grasping man, and choose none of his ways. For the perverse are an abomination [extremely disgusting and detestable] to the Lord** (vv. 31-32, AMP).

You see, "unscrupulousness" is perverted integrity. It is the opposite of what we are to walk in if we want to live in pleasantness and peace. We are to choose none of the ways of those who walk in opposition to justice and integrity, because they are an abomination to the Lord. His face is turned against them.

On the other hand, look at God's wonderful promise to those who walk uprightly in His wisdom: **His confidential communion and secret counsel are with the [uncompromisingly] righteous (those who are upright and in right standing with Him)** (v. 32, AMP).

This passage of Scripture goes on to contrast the homes of the wicked and the righteous: **The curse of the Lord is in and on the house of the wicked, but He declares blessed (joyful and favored with blessings) the home of the just and consistently righteous** (v. 33, AMP).

You can see what walking in the wisdom, reverence and honor of God will do for you in your life. This scripture promises that the more place you give God in your life, the more blessed your home and family will be. God's wisdom is what works!

Then the contrast between the wise and the wicked is taken one more step: **The wise shall inherit glory (all honor and good) but shame is the highest rank conferred on [self-confident] fools** (v. 35, AMP).

I'm telling you, the more we read the Word, the more we can see why we should make wisdom our quest in life! We should use all our ability to pursue the wisdom and knowledge of God. Every blessing we ever receive from God to help us live a worthwhile life has its source in His wisdom!

Wisdom for Today

Acknowledge God in all of your ways today.

*Walk in lovingkindness toward others. Be quick to forgive,
quick to bless, quick to help.*

*When God shows you an area in your life that isn't in line with the Word,
simply receive His chastening and make the necessary correction.*

CHAPTER 4
Wisdom Is the Principal Thing

As you attend to God's Word, His wisdom becomes integrated into the very center of your being, the motivator and the decision-maker of your life.

✦

Proverbs Chapter 4

1 Hear, ye children, the instruction of a father, and attend to know understanding.

2 For I give you good doctrine, forsake ye not my law.

3 For I was my father's son, tender and only beloved in the sight of my mother.

4 He taught me also, and said unto me, Let thine heart retain my words: keep my commandments, and live.

5 Get wisdom, get understanding: forget it not; neither decline from the words of my mouth.

6 Forsake her not, and she shall preserve thee: love her, and she shall keep thee.

7 Wisdom is the principal thing; therefore get wisdom: and with all thy getting get understanding.

8 Exalt her, and she shall promote thee: she shall bring thee to honour, when thou dost embrace her.

9 She shall give to thine head an ornament of grace: a crown of glory shall she deliver to thee.

10 Hear, O my son, and receive my sayings; and the years of thy life shall be many.

11 I have taught thee in the way of wisdom; I have led thee in right paths.

12 When thou goest, thy steps shall not be straitened; and when thou runnest, thou shalt not stumble.

13 Take fast hold of instruction; let her not go: keep her; for she is thy life.

14 Enter not into the path of the wicked, and go not in the way of evil men.

15 Avoid it, pass not by it, turn from it, and pass away.

16 For they sleep not, except they have done mischief; and their sleep is taken away, unless they cause some to fall.

17 For they eat the bread of wickedness, and drink the wine of violence.

18 But the path of the just is as the shining light, that shineth more and more unto the perfect day.

19 The way of the wicked is as darkness: they know not at what they stumble.

20 My son, attend to my words; incline thine ear unto my sayings.

21 Let them not depart from thine eyes; keep them in the midst of thine heart.

22 For they are life unto those that find them, and health to all their flesh.

23 Keep thy heart with all diligence; for out of it are the issues of life.

24 Put away from thee a froward mouth, and perverse lips put far from thee.

25 Let thine eyes look right on, and let thine eyelids look straight before thee.

26 Ponder the path of thy feet, and let all thy ways be established.

27 Turn not to the right hand nor to the left: remove thy foot from evil.

Hidden Treasures

Proverbs 4 is a very important chapter, not only in the book of Proverbs but also in the entire Bible. It holds the key to divine health, to divine prosperity and to walking in the spirit at all times.

This key can be summarized in two words — *get wisdom:* **The beginning of Wisdom is: get Wisdom (skillful and godly Wisdom)! [For *skillful and godly Wisdom is the principal thing.*] And with all you have gotten, get understanding (discernment, comprehension, and interpretation)** (v. 7, AMP).

God says that His wisdom is the *principal* thing. That word "principal" means *first in importance.* Why is wisdom so important?

Proverbs 4:6 (AMP) gives us one answer: **Forsake not [Wisdom], and *she will keep, defend, and protect you;* love her, and she will guard you.** Wisdom keeps, defends and protects us from the evil strategies of our enemy — Satan.

But here's the main reason wisdom is first in importance: When you have God's wisdom, you have the key to everything else.

Solomon understood this. When he was a young man about to become king, God asked him, "What do you want Me to do for you?"

Solomon replied, "I want wisdom. I want to know how to judge these people wisely. I don't know how to go out or come in unless the Lord tells me" (1 Kings 3:7-9, author's paraphrase).

Because Solomon was humble and asked only for wisdom, God gave him not only a wise and understanding heart, but riches and honor as well.

But later Solomon didn't hold fast to wisdom. He went after heathen women, bringing them into his household.

Solomon, the wisest of all men, had the ability to walk with God and follow His ways. He knew what was right. He could have followed after his father David, a man after God's own heart (1 Samuel 13:14). David made mistakes, but he quickly repented and restored his fellowship with God.

But when Solomon went astray, he didn't return to walking in God's way, and the consequences of his sin affected not only himself and his own descendants, but the future generations of an entire nation.

So let that be a lesson to you. You may know the wisdom of God; you may have the ability to walk in the wisdom of God. But even then, you can still choose to go your own way.

It's no different with us than it was with Solomon. We choose. Do we want to go our own way and be cursed with the world? Or do we want to follow God and be blessed?

Exalt Wisdom

God tells us what we are to do with wisdom once we obtain it: *Prize Wisdom highly and exalt her*, **and she will exalt and promote you; she will bring you to honor when you embrace her** (Proverbs 4:8, AMP).

If you want to be promoted in life, this verse tells you the way to do it. Prize wisdom highly and exalt her, and she will exalt and promote you. In other words, go after wisdom and do what wisdom says. Make your life and your decisions revolve around the wisdom of God.

When you do that, wisdom will promote you. She will bring you honor when you embrace her, fulfilling what God has promised: **Those who honor Me I will honor** (1 Samuel 2:30, AMP).

Led in Paths of Uprightness

We've been talking a lot about wisdom, but here's a good definition of what wisdom is: **I have taught you in the way of skillful and godly Wisdom [which is** *comprehensive insight into the ways and purposes of God*]**; I have led you in paths of uprightness** (Proverbs 4:11, AMP).

When you have comprehensive insight into the ways and purposes of God, and you are walking in those ways, then you are walking in wisdom. You are in a position for God to lead you in paths of uprightness.

God tells you what kind of help you can expect as you walk His paths: **When you walk, your steps shall not be hampered [your path will be clear and open]; and when you run, you shall not stumble** (v. 12, AMP).

I read in Maclaren's *Expositions of Holy Scripture* an interesting explanation of this verse. Maclaren explained that the phrase "when you walk" refers to our daily walk with God.[1]

You see, most of our lives are not lived in the spectacular. We live in the daily routine of things. But our everyday lives aren't supposed to be a monotonous drudgery. God is saying that with His wisdom, we can be blessed as we walk through that daily routine. We can be at peace and prosperous no matter what we're doing.

Then Maclaren makes the point that the phrase "when you run" in verse 12 refers to those times in our lives when something spectacular occurs or a significant milestone takes place. In those special times when extra momentum may be required to achieve something great, wisdom says, "As you run with Me, you won't stumble." I like that!

So whether we're living our everyday lives or getting ready to achieve a milestone in our lives, God's wisdom will lead us on the paths of uprightness. It will keep us from falling or stumbling. Our path will be clear and open, and our steps will not be hindered.

Learn To Flow With God

We can see why wisdom is so important for us to have in both the big and the small events of our lives. That's why God exhorts us to **take firm hold of instruction, do not let go; guard her,** *for she is your life* (v. 13, AMP).

Notice, you are to *take fast hold* of God's instruction. That lets you know that a weak, halfhearted hold just isn't going to work. You'll never be able to walk in wisdom and be a "wimpy Christian"!

Why not? Because the whole world is trying to pull you in a direction contrary to God's direction. The world goes one way, and God goes the other way. God's way brings blessing, and the world's way brings a curse. And if you don't take fast hold of God's instruction, you'll be swept away by what the world says and believes.

So hold fast to God's wisdom, knowing that it is your life. Learn to flow with God as a way of life so you aren't swept away by the deadly currents of the world.

---

[1] Alexander Maclaren, D.D., Litt. D., *Expositions of Holy Scripture*, (Grand Rapids: Baker Book House, 1984), Vol. 3, pp. 101-107.

I once read a definition of the word "flow" that used a stick flowing down a river as an example. That's the way we're supposed to flow with God. You see, because we're God's children, a river of His blessings and His will surrounds our lives. All we have to do is just act like that stick floating down the river. We just need to lean not on our own understanding, acknowledge Him in all of our ways and then flow down the current of God's will and His wisdom until we arrive at the destiny He has planned for us.

You know, you may not think you can do a lot of things, but I know you can be like a stick! You can spend time with God in His Word and in prayer until you get to the place where you can hear Him. And then day by day, one step at a time, you can flow with Him the way a stick flows down a river. Let His momentum take you where He wants you to go. Then when you come to the end of your spiritual race and finish your God-appointed course, you will receive the crown of righteousness that God has laid up for those who love Him (2 Timothy 4:7-8).

Avoid the Path of the Wicked

Proverbs 4:14-19 contrasts the clear and open path of the upright with the path of the wicked. For example, **the way of the wicked is like deep darkness; they do not know over what they stumble** (v. 19, AMP).

Now, the path of the wicked isn't the path that your heart (your spirit man) wants to take. The Holy Spirit dwells within you to lead and guide you. Therefore, the natural thing for you to do is to walk with God.

So Satan tries to figure out a way to pull you off the path you know is right. That's why he uses various temptations to solicit you to evil, including people around you who are living in sin. People like that often want to pull you into sin because your righteousness is an affront to them (v. 16). They would feel less convicted if you would join in with them.

So how do you keep from being pulled onto the path of evil? You **avoid it, do not go on it; turn from it and pass on** (v. 15, AMP). In other words, you do what James 4:7 says: **Submit yourselves therefore to God. Resist the devil, and he will flee from you.**

Just keep yourself riveted on the path of the righteous, no matter what Satan throws at you to pull you off. That's the path that **is like the light of dawn, that shines more and more (brighter and clearer) until [it reaches its full strength and glory in] the perfect day [to be prepared]** (Proverbs 4:18, AMP). You can live in the light of God's wisdom in the midst of a very dark world!

Attend to God's Words

Proverbs 4:20-23 is one of my favorite passages of Scripture in the entire Bible. I teach on these verses quite frequently, because they show us *how* to walk with God so that His Word and His wisdom are continually being made life and health to our flesh. This is divine wisdom for divine health!

The first step is pay attention to God's words: **My son, attend to my words; incline thine ear unto my sayings** (v. 20). "To attend" means *to give attention to*. For example, if you were a nurse attending to a patient, you would have to give your full attention to taking care of his needs.

Well, in order to get anywhere in our walk with God, we will have to give Him our full attention. We aren't going to hear Him if our attention is focused on something else. He's a Gentleman; He won't force Himself on us.

Wisdom will cry aloud, but if you don't hear her instruction, you'll suffer the consequences. And you *won't* hear God's wisdom if you don't give Him your attention.

So *how* do we attend to God's words? First, we are to *incline our ear* to the Word (v. 20). Then we must keep on hearing God's Word: **Let them not depart from thine eyes; keep them in the midst of thine heart** (v. 21).

You are to keep the Word coming in through your ears and your eyes so it stays in your heart. You see, you'll forget what the Word says if you don't constantly feed on it.

But as you hear the Word and keep it in front of your eyes, it becomes integrated into the very center of your being; it becomes an inseparable part of you. And as it becomes the motivator and the decision-maker of your life, you begin to walk **securely and in confident trust...without fear or dread of evil** (Proverbs 1:33, AMP).

Keep the Word
In the Midst of Your Heart

Do you want the Word to become life, and healing, and health to all your flesh (Proverbs 4:22, AMP)? Well, the way you stay healed and whole, not only in your physical body but in every area of your life, is to keep the Word in the midst of your heart. How? By attending to God's Word. By keeping it in front of your eyes and going into your ears.

When Ken and I first started "inclining our ears" to God's Word, we listened to reel-to-reel teaching tapes. We listened to those tapes day and night until the Word was deposited in our hearts in abundance. Then we learned that hearing the Word wasn't a one-time proposition. We had to *keep* that Word in the midst of our hearts by giving attention to the Word continually.

You see, you just can't let your faith take a vacation; you have to keep your faith strong. The only way to do that is to continually cause it to come into your ears and to keep it before your eyes. Romans 10:17 says that faith comes by hearing and hearing.

That's basically what God told Joshua to do. God said to Joshua, "Keep My Word in your mouth, and meditate on it day and night so that you do it! Then you will have good success" (Joshua 1:8, author's paraphrase).

Joshua had to *keep* God's Word, *talk* God's Word, *meditate* God's Word and continually act on God's Word. In other words, he had to keep the Word of God in the midst of his heart where it could talk to him.

The Issues of Life

You'll have to keep God's Word in the midst of your heart if you're going to fulfill the next verse: **Keep and guard your heart with all vigilance and above all that you guard, for out of it flow the springs** [forces or issues] **of life** (Proverbs 4:23, AMP).

Let's find out what these forces or issues of life are that keep your heart full of God. These are the divine forces that make your life worth living: **The fruit of the Spirit is love, joy, peace, longsuffering** [patience], **gentleness, goodness, faith** [faithfulness], **meekness, temperance** [self-control]: **against such there is no law** (Galatians 5:22-23).

The fruit of the spirit help you walk in victory. If any of these forces of life are *not* manifested in your life, then in that area you have a weakness. The devil will target that weak area of your life so he can defeat you.

For instance, if you have developed every fruit of the spirit except self-control, then the devil will use your lack of discipline to hinder you. Self-control is a spiritual force that was given to help you keep yourself disciplined and your body under control so you can fulfill your God-given responsibilities.

Patience is a spiritual force that will keep you steady even under severe test and trial. It's the power that undergirds your faith. Patience doesn't yield to circumstances and will keep you from giving up. It doesn't quit, no matter what's happening in your life.

All the spiritual forces God has given us are powerful. And if you will stay in living contact with God through His Word and in prayer, they will all issue forth from your heart like a fountain.

God gave me a picture once of what these issues or outgoings of the Spirit are like in our lives. I was in the Philippines getting ready to conduct a healing service, thinking about this very subject. I happened to look out of my hotel window, and I saw in the plaza below a beautiful, huge fountain shooting water high in the air.

Then God spoke to my spirit, saying, "You can't put trash in the opening where the water gushes out when water is coming out of that fountain. The water will wash away the trash.

"And if the volume of water was turned up so high that the fountain spouted into the air, the force of the water would be so strong, no trash could even get close to the opening."

The Lord continued, "That's the way you are to be in the realm of the Spirit. The issues of life should overflow from your heart in such a great measure that nothing of the world can enter into your spirit, soul or body to contaminate it."

That illustration helped me see that in order to keep things going well in our lives, we are to maintain a constant overflow of these spiritual forces of God's life. As we spend time with God and give Him our attention, those issues of life that come from God and His Word will keep our bodies well. Proverbs 4:22 teaches us how to get well and how to stay well. Take God's Word like medicine! For they (God's words) will also keep our thinking straight. And they will keep us strong and aggressive to walk in the wisdom of God in every area of life.

We read earlier that you find favor with God and man when you bind truth and lovingkindness about your neck and let those qualities become a part of you (Proverbs 3:3-4). Well, the same is true with these spiritual forces issuing out of your heart. They produce supernatural favor in your life as well.

People love to be around someone who is full of love, joy and peace. They love to be around a person who is patient and gentle.

You can see how guarding your heart and allowing these forces of life to flow forth from you gives you favor with others. Besides that, you are so much happier yourself when you are joyful and patient!

Walking in love and joy improves your personality 150 percent. It makes you more personable. It makes people want to be around you.

The fruit of the spirit come forth from your heart. In fact, everything supernatural that you receive from God proceeds out of your heart — *everything*. That's where the Holy Spirit lives. That's where your deposit of the Word is. That's why you have to keep your heart pure and full of God.

You can't play around with the world's sin and expect to walk in these issues of life. You have to honor God and give Him first place. You must let Him have full reign in your heart and give the Word your full attention. You must talk to Him in prayer, listening for His confidential communion and secret counsel, which is so necessary if you want to walk free on this earth (Proverbs 3:32, AMP).

So make wisdom the principal thing in your life. Incline your ear to God's Word, and keep it ever before your eyes. Above all else, guard your heart diligently, for out of it flow all of the divine forces of the life of God to bring you victory and make life worth living!

Wisdom for Today

When the enemy's solicitation to evil comes, don't fellowship with it, think about it or even consider it. Turn away from it and move on!

Deposit an abundance of God's Word in your heart today. Find time to hear the Word, meditate on the Word and talk the Word.

Guard your heart — and let the issues of God's life overflow out of your spirit!

CHAPTER 5
Drink From Your Own Cistern

*God has reserved great rewards for those who
"drink from their own cistern" and
find joy in the person they married.*

Proverbs Chapter 5

1 My son, attend unto my wisdom, and bow thine ear to my understanding:

2 That thou mayest regard discretion, and that thy lips may keep knowledge.

3 For the lips of a strange woman drop as an honeycomb, and her mouth is smoother than oil:

4 But her end is bitter as wormwood, sharp as a twoedged sword.

5 Her feet go down to death; her steps take hold on hell.

6 Lest thou shouldest ponder the path of life, her ways are moveable, that thou canst not know them.

7 Hear me now therefore, O ye children, and depart not from the words of my mouth.

8 Remove thy way far from her, and come not nigh the door of her house:

9 Lest thou give thine honour unto others, and thy years unto the cruel:

10 Lest strangers be filled with thy wealth; and thy labours be in the house of a stranger;

11 And thou mourn at the last, when thy flesh and thy body are consumed,

12 And say, How have I hated instruction, and my heart despised reproof;

13 And have not obeyed the voice of my teachers, nor inclined mine ear to them that instructed me!

14 I was almost in all evil in the midst of the congregation and assembly.

15 Drink waters out of thine own cistern, and running waters out of thine own well.

16 Let thy fountains be dispersed abroad, and rivers of waters in the streets.

17 Let them be only thine own, and not strangers' with thee.

18 Let thy fountain be blessed: and rejoice with the wife of thy youth.

19 Let her be as the loving hind and pleasant roe; let her breasts satisfy thee at all times; and be thou ravished always with her love.

20 And why wilt thou, my son, be ravished with a strange woman, and embrace the bosom of a stranger?

21 For the ways of man are before the eyes of the Lord, and he pondereth all his goings.

22 His own iniquities shall take the wicked himself, and he shall be holden with the cords of his sins.

23 He shall die without instruction; and in the greatness of his folly he shall go astray.

Hidden Treasures

Proverbs 5 is one of several warnings on the dangers of adultery found in the book of Proverbs. This chapter also provides God's solution for married people so they can avoid this path that leads only to destruction.

The chapter begins by exhorting you to be attentive to God's wisdom **that you may exercise proper discrimination and discretion and your lips may guard and keep knowledge and the wise answer [to temptation]** (v. 2, AMP).

If you're married or are planning to get married someday, you definitely need proper discrimination and discretion in today's society when it comes to relating to the opposite sex.

Why? Because two sins of the flesh that Satan uses in the world to gain control over people are sexual immorality and adultery. Actually, these two sins are at the top of his list.

The world pushes adultery through the media and books as if it were no more dangerous than eating an ice cream cone. Just turn on your television set, and there it is. It's as if people are committing adultery seven days a week, on every channel, all the time! The underlying message is clear: "Come on, everybody does it. Nothing is wrong with adultery. It's just no big deal."

But that's a lie. All you have to do is study the Word, and you'll quickly discover God's perspective on the subject: Sin will kill you — and adultery is one of the biggest killers!

Adultery steals your happiness. It destroys your marriage. It ruins other people's lives. It's one of the most dangerous temptations a man or a woman can ever yield to, deadlier than a rattlesnake. The Bible warns that the feet of the adulteress **go down to death; her steps take hold of Sheol (Hades, the place of the dead)** (v. 5, AMP).

Ken and I have seen men and women of God who knew the Word get drawn into adultery. Just like you, they probably thought it could never happen to them, but it did. So beware — adultery isn't a lightweight temptation. It is never something to fool around with, because the person who commits adultery **loses sight of and walks not in the path of life** (v. 6, AMP).

Don't Put It Off —
Avoid Temptation

❦

We would do well to remember what God said in Proverbs 4:26-27 (AMP) in light of this subject of adultery: **Consider well the path of your feet, and let all your ways be established and ordered aright. Turn not aside to the right hand or to the left; remove your foot from evil.**

We might be surprised at how much heartache and trouble can be prevented in lives by taking this wise counsel!

Let's say you're a married man with a wife and children at home, and a good-looking woman at work begins telling you how wonderful and handsome you are. What do you do in a situation like that? You let discretion rise up within you and say, "You're already almost in trouble. Avoid this woman." Then you **remove your foot from evil** and get out of that situation as quickly as you can!

Why is that type of situation so dangerous? Because often married life can seem to become monotonous and unexciting. For example, when the husband gets up in the morning, maybe his wife doesn't tell him how wonderful he is. She may not even talk much to him at the breakfast table. She may be too busy getting her children ready for school or getting ready to go to work, doing what a busy mother is expected to do.

Then the husband goes to the workplace and interacts with a good-looking young woman who is looking for a husband and doesn't care if the one she finds already has a wife. This girl is looking for a home. She begins to flatter him, telling him how smart and handsome he is. And if he believes her words, he's going to be in trouble! He may think, *My wife never tells me that. In fact, she tells me everything I do wrong.*

That's how the devil's trap is sprung. I'm warning you, don't go for it!

So what if you're married and you begin to get too close to someone of the opposite sex? The very first time wisdom and discretion rise up in you and say, *You're getting too friendly with this person,* immediately shut the door on the relationship. Don't wait and say, "Well, I'm not doing anything wrong. I'm just enjoying the fellowship of this person." Don't let the situation go on until it becomes a bigger problem.

Let discretion rise up within you and remind you, *Hey, I'm married. I love my spouse. I love the Lord. I'm going to walk in God's ways of wisdom and avoid this trap before I get into trouble!*

I'm telling you, you can't afford to even flirt around with the thought of adultery. It's an extremely strong and dangerous force. Just turn away from the path of evil. Follow wisdom's counsel: **Avoid the very scenes of temptation** (Proverbs 5:8, AMP).

You don't have any business enjoying someone else's company of the opposite sex if your spouse isn't there with you. You're playing a deadly game, and the consequences are terrible to consider.

Look at some of those consequences: **Lest you give your honor to others and your years to those without mercy.... And you groan and mourn when your end comes** (vv. 9,11, AMP).

The Bible also talks about the honor of intimacy that should be reserved only for your spouse: **Marriage is honourable in all, and the bed undefiled: but whoremongers and adulterers God will judge** (Hebrews 13:4).

I hope you're getting an idea of how serious the sin of adultery is to God. He expects the marriage covenant to be honored.

Wisdom's Instructions to the Married

So here are wisdom's instructions to us: **Drink waters out of your own cistern [of a pure marriage relationship], and fresh running waters out of your own well** (Proverbs 5:15, AMP). We are to fully enjoy our relationship with our own spouse.

That scripture is also God's answer to AIDS. The world has no answer to AIDS, but wisdom does: **Drink waters out of your own cistern.**

The Bible goes on to say, **Let your fountain [of human life] be blessed [with the rewards of fidelity], and** *rejoice in the wife of your youth* (v. 18, AMP). According to this scripture, God has reserved great rewards for those who "drink from their own cistern." And one of those rewards is finding joy in the person they married!

God has a very good reason for telling us to avoid every temptation to commit adultery. He doesn't want us to be like the adulterer: **His own iniquities shall ensnare the wicked man, and he shall be held with the cords of**

his sin. He will die for lack of discipline and instruction, and in the greatness of his folly he will go astray and be lost (vv. 22-23, AMP).

God wants us free. He wants us delivered. That's why He tells us to find joy in the marriage covenant as we stay faithful to our spouse.

God sets us in families. God Himself is family oriented. If you have no family; here is a scripture for you: **God places the solitary in families and gives the desolate a home in which to dwell...** (Psalm 68:6, AMP).

God wanted a family around Him, so He created man and woman and told them to be fruitful and multiply. He said He will bless our seed — our family. God has purposed that one man and one woman come together in marriage and produce sons and daughters to surround them all of their days. And "the gift goes on" — grandchildren, great-grandchildren. There is no end to blessing in the families of God. Each generation should be stronger. There is no blessing greater than a family. Faithfulness to the marriage covenant keeps the family intact.

Wisdom for Today

*Don't feed your mind (through television, movies, books, etc.) on the
world's message that "adultery is no big deal."
Don't even toy around with the thought of adultery.
Make the decision to give honor to the one you married
by staying faithful.*

CHAPTER 6
Divine Reproofs of Discipline

As disciples of Jesus Christ, we are to heed and obey
God's reproofs of discipline. This is to be our way of life,
for every divine reproof is given only for our good.

❦

Proverbs Chapter 6

1   My son, if thou be surety for thy friend, if thou hast stricken thy hand with a stranger,

2   Thou art snared with the words of thy mouth, thou art taken with the words of thy mouth.

3   Do this now, my son, and deliver thyself, when thou art come into the hand of thy friend; go, humble thyself, and make sure thy friend.

4   Give not sleep to thine eyes, nor slumber to thine eyelids.

5   Deliver thyself as a roe from the hand of the hunter, and as a bird from the hand of the fowler.

6   Go to the ant, thou sluggard; consider her ways, and be wise:

7   Which having no guide, overseer, or ruler,

8   Provideth her meat in the summer, and gathereth her food in the harvest.

9   How long wilt thou sleep, O sluggard? when wilt thou arise out of thy sleep?

10   Yet a little sleep, a little slumber, a little folding of the hands to sleep:

11   So shall thy poverty come as one that travelleth, and thy want as an armed man.

12   A naughty person, a wicked man, walketh with a froward mouth.

13   He winketh with his eyes, he speaketh with his feet, he teacheth with his fingers;

14   Frowardness is in his heart, he deviseth mischief continually; he soweth discord.

15   Therefore shall his calamity come suddenly; suddenly shall he be broken without remedy.

16   These six things doth the Lord hate: yea, seven are an abomination unto him:

17   A proud look, a lying tongue, and hands that shed innocent blood,

18   An heart that deviseth wicked imaginations, feet that be swift in running to mischief,

19   A false witness that speaketh lies, and he that soweth discord among brethren.

20   My son, keep thy father's commandment, and forsake not the law of thy mother:

21   Bind them continually upon thine heart, and tie them about thy neck.

22   When thou goest, it shall lead thee; when thou sleepest, it shall keep thee; and when thou awakest, it shall talk with thee.

23   For the commandment is a lamp; and the law is light; and reproofs of instruction are the way of life:

24 To keep thee from the evil woman, from the flattery of the tongue of a strange woman.

25 Lust not after her beauty in thine heart; neither let her take thee with her eyelids.

26 For by means of a whorish woman a man is brought to a piece of bread: and the adulteress will hunt for the precious life.

27 Can a man take fire in his bosom, and his clothes not be burned?

28 Can one go upon hot coals, and his feet not be burned?

29 So he that goeth in to his neighbour's wife; whosoever toucheth her shall not be innocent.

30 Men do not despise a thief, if he steal to satisfy his soul when he is hungry;

31 But if he be found, he shall restore sevenfold; he shall give all the substance of his house.

32 But whoso committeth adultery with a woman lacketh understanding: he that doeth it destroyeth his own soul.

33 A wound and dishonour shall he get; and his reproach shall not be wiped away.

34 For jealousy is the rage of a man: therefore he will not spare in the day of vengeance.

35 He will not regard any ransom; neither will he rest content, though thou givest many gifts.

Hidden Treasures

Proverbs 6:23 tells us that God's Word serves as a lamp to light our path through life, revealing the right way to go. The wisdom of God causes us to walk in His light instead of in the darkness of this world. With the light of God's Word, we can walk in His blessings instead of under the curse of the law.

Included in God's wisdom are reproofs of discipline that help us avoid the many pitfalls along the way. These divine reproofs of discipline are to be our way of life (v. 23).

You see, it's not enough to be born again into the kingdom of God. God also expects us to become disciples. That's why Jesus didn't say we were to go into all the world and get people born again. He told us to go and teach all nations, *making disciples* (Matthew 28:19).

A disciple of the Lord Jesus Christ is simply one who is disciplined by what Jesus teaches and commands. The disciple is quick to heed and to obey the Lord's reproofs of discipline.

Let's take a look at the divine reproofs of discipline found in Proverbs 6.

Don't Become Security for Your Neighbor

If you follow God's counsel in verses 1-5, you are going to save yourself a great deal of money. This passage of Scripture is talking about becoming security for someone else's debts. The wisdom of God is sending a clear message: "Don't do it!"

If you have become security for someone, or cosigned for them, **you are snared with the words of your lips** (v. 2, AMP). So what do you do if someone comes to you and says, "Please sign my note so I can borrow this money?" Just say, "I'm sorry, I can't do that. The wisdom of God has admonished me not to become security for someone."

Now, this scripture isn't telling you not to help a friend by loaning him money. But it *is* saying that you shouldn't promise to pay his debts.

More than likely, your friend needs someone to cosign for him because he got himself in financial trouble in the past. If that's true, there is a good chance that he might get into another financial bind in the future. And if you become security for him, you may very well end up paying his debt.

So what are wisdom's instructions to you if you have snared yourself with the words of your lips and **put yourself into the power of your neighbor** (v. 3, AMP)?

First, don't waste any time in dealing with the problem. Instead, **Do this now [at once and earnestly], my son, and deliver yourself...go, bestir and humble yourself, and beg your neighbor [to pay his debt and thereby release you]** (v. 3, AMP). Meanwhile, believe God for His help in getting out of the mess you've made for yourself.

Don't Be a Sluggard

Verse 6 starts a new discourse on the foolishness of a sluggard. If you want to know how to become poor, here's how you do it: **Yet a little sleep, a little slumber, a little folding of the hands to lie down and sleep — So will your poverty come like a robber or one who travels [with slowly but surely approaching steps] and your want like an armed man [making you helpless]** (vv. 10-11, AMP).

So don't let the label "sluggard" become attached to you — get up and do something about your situation!

The Bible says that **slothfulness casts one into a deep sleep, and the idle person shall suffer hunger** (Proverbs 19:15, AMP). If you think you can be lazy and still prosper, you're fooling yourself. Now, you may marry someone who isn't lazy and let your spouse prosper you. But that won't fulfill you as a person.

Slothfulness is an enemy. It keeps you from fulfilling God's destiny that He has planned for you.

If you aren't moving on with God — if you don't have God-given goals and dreams in your heart that you are striving to accomplish — then you can just be sure of this: You're going to stay unhappy and unfulfilled because God made you to increase and grow.

He has a plan for every one of us to follow. Listen to this: **"For I know the plans I have for you," declares the Lord, "plans to prosper you and not to harm you, plans to give you hope and a future"** (Jeremiah 29:11, NIV).

So don't be a slothful, lazy person with no initiative or drive to change what needs to be changed. Listen to what wisdom is saying to you: **Awake thou that sleepest, and arise from the dead** (Ephesians 5:14). Do whatever it takes to walk in God's wisdom and fulfill His plan for your life.

Don't Sow Discord Among Brethren

Proverbs 6:12-15 describes someone you don't want to be: **A worthless person, a wicked man, is he who goes about with a perverse (contrary, wayward) mouth** (v. 12, AMP).

This person is not only contrary with his mouth, he's contrary in his heart, devising **trouble, vexation, and evil continually; he lets loose discord and sows it** (v. 14, AMP).

Sowing discord is serious business to God. God hates **he who sows discord among his brethren** (v. 19 AMP). Therefore, the outcome of the person with a perverse or undisciplined mouth, who says things he shouldn't and causes strife, contention and trouble, is that **suddenly shall he be broken, and that without remedy** (v. 15, AMP).

You will never have any satisfaction in life if you sow discord, because wisdom says the result of that kind of lifestyle is calamity. You'll cause trouble wherever you go.

The Bible says we are to be *peacemakers*, not *discord-sowers* (Matthew 5:9). So take heed to this divine reproof of discipline. Make sure *you* aren't one of these willful, contrary people God is talking about!

Adultery — Don't Touch It!

Once again, the book of Proverbs gives us another warning about the sin of adultery (Proverbs 6:24-35). Wisdom seems to be very concerned that we get the message about the danger of this sin! That's why I'm putting special emphasis on this subject as we go through these first several chapters of Proverbs.

In Proverbs, the woman is referred to as the adulteress who seduces the man. But we know that it works both ways.

For instance, when the Pharisees brought to Jesus the woman whom they had caught in the very act of adultery, she was alone (John 8:3-11). But a woman can't be caught in the act of adultery unless she is with someone else. That woman brought before Jesus was *not* the only guilty party!

In this particular passage about adultery, I want to focus on the following verse: **Whoever commits adultery with a woman lacks heart and understanding (moral principle and prudence);** *he who does it is destroying his own life* (Proverbs 6:32, AMP).

All sin has consequences. Sin always brings death — the death of your fellowship with God, the death of God's blessings in your life, maybe even physical death. But some sins are more dangerous than others, and adultery is one of the most dangerous. It results in more serious consequences than almost any other sin.

It's clear from the Word that there is more to adultery than just a moment of sin. If you're ever tempted with adultery, I want you to remember what I'm telling you. It steals and destroys life. Adultery is a killer. Don't bring it into your family.

We can see an example of the deadly consequences of adultery in the life of King David (2 Samuel 11-12). After David committed adultery with Bathsheba, their infant son conceived from that union became sick. And even though David repented of his sin, certain consequences had already been set into motion.

You see, no one is ever pulled into adultery completely unaware. People who commit adultery know they are doing wrong when they do it. But when lust rises up, they decide to yield to it.

Sometimes people think, *Well, I'll just do it this once. I can always repent and receive forgiveness later.*

But with some sins, you set certain things into motion that stay in motion even after you receive forgiveness — things that can hurt your life, confuse your mind and cause hurt to the people around you. And you may have to deal with those consequences for years and years to come.

In David's case, he repented and God forgave him because His mercy is so great. In the years that followed, David continued to be a man after God's heart. God even honored David in many ways after that incident.

But through David's act of adultery and his part in the death of Bathsheba's husband, Uriah, something had been set in motion that could not be stopped. And when David's child became sick, he couldn't get him healed no matter how much he fasted and prayed. David did not die, but the death of Uriah and David's son were the direct result of David's adultery with Bathsheba.

Adultery truly is a killer. Of course, we know that adultery doesn't always bring physical death quickly. If that were true, this earth would be a lot less populated! But I think you can always expect very serious consequences. Based on God's Word, I can assure you that it is a dangerous, deadly thing to do. So whatever you do, don't touch it!

Reproof for Our Good

You'll find God's reproofs of discipline scattered throughout the book of Proverbs. Whenever you read one of those reproofs, remember — when God reproves, it is only for your benefit. That's why He said that His reproofs of discipline are the way of life (v. 23, AMP).

So be a good disciple of Jesus Christ — take heed and obey the Father's reproofs of love!

Wisdom for Today

If someone asks you to become security for his debts, just say no!

*Get up and do something about fulfilling
the dreams God has placed in your heart.*

*Set spiritual laws of life into motion by heeding
and obeying the wisdom of God.*

CHAPTER 7
God's Unchanging Word

If you will put God's Word on deposit in your spirit, it will be there when you come up against a trial or temptation. God's wisdom will give you guidance and help when you don't know what to do.

❦

Proverbs Chapter 7

1   My son, keep my words, and lay up my commandments with thee.

2   Keep my commandments, and live; and my law as the apple of thine eye.

3   Bind them upon thy fingers, write them upon the table of thine heart.

4   Say unto wisdom, Thou art my sister; and call understanding thy kinswoman:

5   That they may keep thee from the strange woman, from the stranger which flattereth with her words.

6   For at the window of my house I looked through my casement,

7   And beheld among the simple ones, I discerned among the youths, a young man void of understanding,

8   Passing through the street near her corner; and he went the way to her house,

9   In the twilight, in the evening, in the black and dark night:

10   And, behold, there met him a woman with the attire of an harlot, and subtil of heart.

11   (She is loud and stubborn; her feet abide not in her house:

12   Now is she without, now in the streets, and lieth in wait at every corner.)

13   So she caught him, and kissed him, and with an impudent face said unto him,

14   I have peace offerings with me; this day have I payed my vows.

15   Therefore came I forth to meet thee, diligently to seek thy face, and I have found thee.

16   I have decked my bed with coverings of tapestry, with carved works, with fine linen of Egypt.

17   I have perfumed my bed with myrrh, aloes, and cinnamon.

18   Come, let us take our fill of love until the morning: let us solace ourselves with loves.

19   For the goodman is not at home, he is gone a long journey:

20   He hath taken a bag of money with him, and will come home at the day appointed.

21   With her much fair speech she caused him to yield, with the flattering of her lips she forced him.

22   He goeth after her straightway, as an ox goeth to the slaughter, or as a fool to the correction of the stocks;

23   Till a dart strike through his liver; as a bird hasteth to the snare, and knoweth not that it is for his life.

24 Hearken unto me now therefore, O ye children, and attend to the words of my mouth.

25 Let not thine heart decline to her ways, go not astray in her paths.

26 For she hath cast down many wounded: yea, many strong men have been slain by her.

27 Her house is the way to hell, going down to the chambers of death.

Hidden Treasures

God never changes, and neither do the principles and laws He has established to govern life. So when we find these divine principles in the Word, we can know that they are truth — the way things really are. With that in mind, let's look at Proverbs 7.

Deposit the Word in Your Heart

First, let's look at the way this chapter begins. Verse 1 holds a hidden treasure of the Word, to be discovered by the discerning heart: **My son, keep my words;** *lay up within you my commandments [for use when needed]* **and treasure them** (AMP).

We are to lay up God's commandments in our hearts for use when we need them. That's such an important principle to understand. If we don't take the time to get into the Word and deposit it into our hearts now, God's wisdom won't be stored there to guide and help us when we need it.

We know from Romans 10:17 that **faith cometh by hearing, and hearing by the word of God.** Now, it's true that when you are born again, faith is born into your spirit. But to activate that faith and cause it to grow, you have to get the Word planted deep in your heart.

Initially, God put the measure of faith in your heart — but you're the only one who can make it increase. You do that by keeping the Word in front of your eyes, in your ears and in your mouth.

If you will put that Word on deposit in your spirit, it will be there when you need it. When you come up against a trial, a temptation or a dangerous situation and you don't know what to do, victory will rise up out of your heart through your mouth. You'll speak words of faith that will cause that impossible situation to disappear before you.

But it's just like money in the bank. If you haven't been making any deposits, don't expect to make any withdrawals.

For example, you probably would never make the mistake of trying to write a $20,000 check with only $20 in your checking account. But in the spirit realm, believers make that very mistake every day because they don't maintain a healthy balance in their spiritual bank account. So when they run into trouble and need to draw on the assets of heaven — such as prosperity, healing and miracles — they come up empty-handed.

But spiritual currency works the same way natural currency works. If you have an abundance in your natural bank account, you can enjoy plenty of material things. And if you have an abundance in your spiritual account, you can enjoy plenty of *everything* — wealth, health, good relationships, peace and success — because the Bible says God **giveth us richly all things to enjoy** (1 Timothy 6:17).

The most important thing you will do each day is to make those faith deposits. Don't just make them in times of crisis either. Make them *before* you need them.

I remember a letter Ken and I received from a family whose child drowned in their swimming pool. When they found that baby in the pool, he had already turned blue and quit breathing.

But because the parents had faithfully deposited the Word of God in their hearts, they were prepared. No one said, "Go look up a scripture." (Sometimes you don't have time to get your Bible. That's why you'd better keep the Word on deposit in your heart at all times. It could save your life or your loved one's life!)

Immediately that family began to pray, rebuking death and commanding the spirit of that baby to come back. As a result, that child is alive and well today!

The Scripture provides another key that will help you deposit the Word in your heart: **Keep my law and teaching as the apple (the pupil) of your eye** (Proverbs 7:2, AMP). That means you are to keep the Word as the focus of your attention.

For example, if sickness tries to attach itself to your body, your first thought shouldn't be about your doctor. Your first thought ought to be that Jesus is your Healer and that by His stripes, you were healed (1 Peter 2:24). In other words, your focus should be on what the *Word* says about your healing, not on your symptoms.

So how much faith is in *your* faith account? Is it enough to produce victory every day of your life? If not, start making some big deposits of the Word in your heart. Keep God's promises in the center of your eye. Write them on the tablet of your heart (v. 3). Jesus said, **If ye abide in me, and my words abide in you, ye shall ask what ye will, and it shall be done unto you** (John 15:7).

Then when you face a problem and it's time to make a withdrawal, speak words of faith. Don't talk the circumstances. Say what *God* says the outcome is going to be. Use your words to write some "checks" on that faith account you've been building. You'll be amazed at the faith victories you'll experience!

God's Wisdom Helps Us
Say No to Temptation

❦

One of the greatest faith challenges we face every day is to overcome temptation. That's why we need an abundance of God's Word on deposit in our hearts.

The Word gives us the wisdom and power we need to say no to Satan's solicitations to evil. Our part is to **regard understanding or insight as your intimate friend — That they may keep you from the loose woman, from the adventuress who flatters with and makes smooth her words** (Proverbs 7:4-5, AMP).

It's amazing how much Proverbs talks about adultery in these first several chapters of Proverbs. Let's talk about this subject one more time in light of God's unchanging Word.

Are God's Views
On Adultery Outdated?

❦

As I said, the modern world says that adultery and sex outside of marriage are all right. The world's attitude is, "Marriage is old-fashioned, and so is God. His ideas are outdated. There isn't anything wrong with adultery or premarital sex. Everyone does it."

But God never changes. His truth never changes. His ways never change.

Sin never changes either. Sin still pays the same wages. Sin always brings death, and it always will. Even if the whole world believes that sin brings no consequences, it won't change sin's outcome.

The world tries to deceive us, because the world is deceived itself. It is following after Satan, the deceiver, and he is deceived as well!

Often worldly people don't even know they are lying to you. They may actually believe that they can get away with immorality. Because they don't know God's truth, the devil's lies are the only reality they are familiar with.

That's why we go to God's Word. We don't base our lives on what we see, on what our neighbors say, nor on what we hear on television. Instead, we keep God's Word in the center of our eyesight. We live and move and have our being according to that Word instead of according to the world around us. We believe what God says.

Remove Ungodly Influences

Through the ages, it's always been important to turn from ungodly influences and focus on God's Word. Think about what God said to Israel when He sent them into the Promised Land. He told them to destroy *all* their enemies who inhabited the land (Exodus 23:24). In fact, the Israelites got into serious trouble with God if they went in and only conquered some of their enemies without destroying all the heathen living there.

Now, God is a good God, and He loves people. He was as full of mercy then as He is today. But He knew that His people couldn't coexist with heathen and still walk in His ways. It was a matter of the survival of His covenant people.

God was also just as merciful when He told Noah to build the ark. God called Noah an upright man in his generation (Genesis 7:1). Sin had so encroached on God's creation that Noah was the only righteous man left on the earth. Only Noah and his family stood between God and the annihilation of mankind. That's how long our merciful God waited to judge sin!

So God had to destroy the sin that ran rampant in the world in order to save those last righteous lives. Otherwise, mankind would have been totally destroyed. Think about it. God waited until only one righteous man and his family were left, and then He had to act. I tell you, the mercy of God is amazing!

God told the Israelites, "When you go into the land, clear it out. Remove all the people who are there." But when the Israelites went into enemy territory, sometimes they didn't utterly destroy the enemy as God had commanded them.

As a result, they eventually began to become like their enemies. The ways of the heathen began to rub off on them. Instead of holding fast to the ways and thoughts of God, the Israelites began to think like the heathen people around them.

Well, God knew they would do that. He knew that the only way they could walk with Him successfully was to annihilate the ungodly in the land. That's why He commanded them to completely destroy all evil influences that would eventually pull their hearts away from Him.

Today we are still under that same kind of strong pressure to conform as the world tries to pull us into its way of thinking. The world's way of thinking is opposite of God's way of thinking. That's why we have to keep the Word before our eyes and in our heart. God's wisdom will keep us from being deceived.

You see, the Spirit of God is the Spirit of Truth (John 16:13). He comes to live in us to teach us truth, and truth is all He will ever teach us.

So what kind of truth does He teach us? The same thing He tried to teach the Israelites: **The grace of God that bringeth salvation hath appeared to all men, teaching us that, denying ungodliness and worldly lusts, we should live soberly, righteously, and godly, in this present world** (Titus 2:11-12).

In other words, it is the favor of God that teaches us to live righteously and to think like God, to act like God and to deny worldly lusts. He doesn't tell us to deny ungodliness so that we won't have any fun. He's trying to help us truly *live*.

Proverbs 7:6-23 tells the story of **a young man void of good sense** (Proverbs 7:7, AMP). This young man doesn't do what wisdom tells him to do. He doesn't deny ungodliness, nor does he avoid the scene of temptation (Proverbs 5:8, AMP.) He lingers near the loose woman's house, and eventually he yields to her seduction. He follows her to the bed of adultery **like a bird fluttering straight into the net [he hastens], not knowing that it will cost him his life** (Proverbs 7:23, AMP).

God's principles never change. Truth is always truth. Adultery still costs people their lives.

So adopt God's perspective on this subject. When the temptation to stray onto the path of adultery looms in front of you, listen to the voice of the Spirit of Grace teaching and admonishing you, "Go God's way instead of the world's way. Deny worldly lusts. Avoid this path of evil."

That warning never changes, because adultery is never acceptable to God. As you heed His warning and turn from this path that leads **to the chambers of death** (v. 27), your obedience will keep you in a position to reap the rewards of the righteous.

Wisdom for Today

*Take the time to get into the Word and make a faith deposit
into your heart, with the Word of God.*

*When you face a problem, don't talk the circumstances, let faith words
come out of your heart. Say what God says the outcome is going to be.*

Base what you believe on what the Word says, not on what the world says.

CHAPTER 8
The Foundation of a Prosperous Life

The foundation of prosperity in every realm of life
is a continual lifestyle built on the Word and the
wisdom of God.

Proverbs Chapter 8

1 Doth not wisdom cry? and understanding put forth her voice?

2 She standeth in the top of high places, by the way in the places of the paths.

3 She crieth at the gates, at the entry of the city, at the coming in at the doors.

4 Unto you, O men, I call; and my voice is to the sons of man.

5 O ye simple, understand wisdom: and, ye fools, be ye of an understanding heart.

6 Hear; for I will speak of excellent things; and the opening of my lips shall be right things.

7 For my mouth shall speak truth; and wickedness is an abomination to my lips.

8 All the words of my mouth are in righteousness; there is nothing froward or perverse in them.

9 They are all plain to him that understandeth, and right to them that find knowledge.

10 Receive my instruction, and not silver; and knowledge rather than choice gold.

11 For wisdom is better than rubies; and all the things that may be desired are not to be compared to it.

12 I wisdom dwell with prudence, and find out knowledge of witty inventions.

13 The fear of the Lord is to hate evil: pride, and arrogancy, and the evil way, and the froward mouth, do I hate.

14 Counsel is mine, and sound wisdom: I am understanding; I have strength.

15 By me kings reign, and princes decree justice.

16 By me princes rule, and nobles, even all the judges of the earth.

17 I love them that love me; and those that seek me early shall find me.

18 Riches and honour are with me; yea, durable riches and righteousness.

19 My fruit is better than gold, yea, than fine gold; and my revenue than choice silver.

20 I lead in the way of righteousness, in the midst of the paths of judgment:

21 That I may cause those that love me to inherit substance; and I will fill their treasures.

22 The Lord possessed me in the beginning of his way, before his works of old.

23 I was set up from everlasting, from the beginning, or ever the earth was.

24 When there were no depths, I was brought forth; when there were no fountains abounding with water.

25 Before the mountains were settled, before the hills was I brought forth:

26 While as yet he had not made the earth, nor the fields, nor the highest part of the dust of the world.

27 When he prepared the heavens, I was there: when he set a compass upon the face of the depth:

28 When he established the clouds above: when he strengthened the fountains of the deep:

29 When he gave to the sea his decree, that the waters should not pass his commandment: when he appointed the foundations of the earth:

30 Then I was by him, as one brought up with him: and I was daily his delight, rejoicing always before him;

31 Rejoicing in the habitable part of his earth; and my delights were with the sons of men.

32 Now therefore hearken unto me, O ye children: for blessed are they that keep my ways.

33 Hear instruction, and be wise, and refuse it not.

34 Blessed is the man that heareth me, watching daily at my gates, waiting at the posts of my doors.

35 For whoso findeth me findeth life, and shall obtain favour of the Lord.

36 But he that sinneth against me wrongeth his own soul: all they that hate me love death.

Hidden Treasures

Once again in Proverbs 8, wisdom stands crying aloud to those who will listen: **Hear, for I will speak excellent and princely things; and the opening of my lips shall be for right things** (v. 6, AMP).

The value of heeding the voice of wisdom is beyond price: **All the things that may be desired are not to be compared to it** (v. 11, AMP). That's because the foundation of prosperity in every realm of life is a continual lifestyle built on the Word and the wisdom of God.

A Lifestyle Based on God's Word

So how do you live a continual lifestyle based on the wisdom of God? Well, whatever God tells you to do in the Scriptures, you do it. If He tells you to think a certain way, you think that way. If He tells you words you should

speak, you speak those words. That kind of obedience is the basis for prospering in God.

Now, it's possible to prosper in the world without God, but only in one aspect of prosperity — that is, money. That's why receiving God's wisdom is **in preference to [striving for] silver, and knowledge rather than choice gold** (Proverbs 8:10, AMP).

You see, money isn't enough to ensure a good life. It certainly helps, but it isn't life itself. It can't give you healing. It won't cause you to prosper in your spirit or your mind or your body.

In fact, many times when people prosper in the world and acquire a great deal of money, it does them more harm than good. Sometimes their wealth can just help them die younger and in more misery than they would have if they had never become rich.

Just look at many of the actors, athletes and other rich, famous people in the world. If they don't know God, they often use their money to indulge in sin without restraint. Some buy all the cocaine they want. Others drink all the alcohol they want. Too many pursue an immoral lifestyle unchecked.

How does that kind of lifestyle affect these so-called "prosperous" people? Well, no matter how much money a person has, sin still pays the same wages: death. No one can get away from that fact.

So when I talk about building a foundation for a prosperous life, I'm not just talking about financial prosperity. That's just a part of our inheritance as children of God. I'm talking about prosperity for the whole man, which includes healing, supernatural peace and mental soundness, as well as financial and material increase and stability.

Building a Foundation of Prosperity

Before God ever created the earth for His family, He set in motion certain laws and principles by which heaven and earth have to abide: **The Lord formed and brought me [Wisdom] forth at the beginning of His way, before His acts of old. I [Wisdom] was inaugurated and ordained from everlasting, from the beginning, before ever the earth existed** (Proverbs 8:22-23, AMP).

God has always wanted to bless His people. And when we build our lives on His principles of wisdom that He has set into motion, we will prosper in every area of our lives.

When God speaks, His power is in His words to bring them to pass. So when we latch onto His words, depositing them in our hearts and mouths and acting on them in faith, we are building a foundation of prosperity to help us live successfully on this earth.

When Ken and I were first born again and filled with the Holy Spirit, we didn't really know anything about God's principles of spiritual prosperity. For instance, we didn't know that healing belonged to us, so we just let sickness stay when it came to our home.

But later we found out that Jesus bore our sicknesses and carried our disease (Isaiah 53:4). We learned how to resist sickness and disease. When sickness came, we began to stand against it in the name of Jesus, saying, "No, you aren't the will of God, and you aren't staying in my body!" or "You aren't staying in my child!" We told sickness that it had to go in Jesus' name!

However, we didn't know to handle poverty and lack the same way. Our financial situation was still the major problem in our lives.

We had learned that financial prosperity was the will of God, but I didn't have the revelation yet to resist poverty as I would sickness.

I remember right where I was the day I received that revelation. We were living in Fort Worth, Texas, and I was looking out the window toward downtown when the Lord spoke to my heart. He revealed to me that we were to talk to lack in the same way we had learned to talk to sickness and disease. So, I said, "Lack, I rebuke you in Jesus' name. Get out of my life! You are not the will of God for me. I resist you in Jesus' name."

God Wants Us to Prosper

I'm telling you, poverty is *not* the will of God. It's a curse, and so is lack! (Deuteronomy 28). God doesn't want you laboring under poverty and lack. He doesn't want your time taken up worrying, *How am I going to pay my light bill?* That's *not* the will of God for you.

It's always been God's desire for His family to prosper. That's why He instructs us in the way of wisdom: **That I may cause those who love me to inherit [true] riches and that I may fill their treasuries** (Proverbs 8:21, AMP).

Wisdom brings us both spiritual and earthly blessings. But we don't apply God's principles just to acquire material wealth. We apply them because He is our God and we want to honor and obey Him in every area.

You can't just say, "Well, I want to prosper, so I'm going to look up all the scriptures on prosperity and ignore everything else in the Word."

No, that won't work. Prospering in God is a lifestyle of doing the Word — all of it! The more we know about God and His wisdom, the easier it is to prosper in Him.

Seek First God and His Wisdom

We saw earlier that **wisdom is better than rubies or pearls** (v. 11, AMP). This scripture says that nothing you can desire compares to skillful and godly wisdom. Nothing!

You see, it's a matter of priorities. God doesn't want us striving after riches; He wants us to seek after His wisdom. As we do that, He promises that all of His other blessings will be added unto us.

That's exactly what Jesus said: **Seek (aim at and strive after) first of all His kingdom and His righteousness (His way of doing and being right), and then all these things taken together will be given you besides** (Matthew 6:33, AMP).

So we see that building a foundation of godly prosperity is the result of living for God and putting His Word first place in our lives. As we seek first after God and His way of doing and being right, we are putting ourselves in a position for increase. That's the only safe way to become prosperous.

That's what happened with Ken and me years ago when we first began our faith walk. We started treating the Word for what it really is — supernatural, alive and energizing with the power in it to bring each promise to pass (Hebrews 4:12, AMP). We put the Word in our mouths and in our hearts. We did what it said to do, whether we wanted to or not.

By doing that, we were seeking first God's kingdom. We were receiving God's instruction **in preference to [striving for] silver, and knowledge rather than choice gold** (Proverbs 8:10, AMP).

Then one day Ken and I found a scripture that said, **Keep out of debt and owe no man anything, except to love one another** (Romans 13:8, AMP). So we made the decision on the basis of God's Word that we were going to get out of debt and never again incur any more debt.

But because we still didn't know much about faith, it seemed to us that that decision would be our doom. (Since then, we've learned that God's Word *always* works to our advantage. But we didn't know it then. We had to learn it during "on-the-job training" in the laboratory of life!)

We thought, *How will we ever get a car or the other things we need without going into debt?* But even though we thought our decision to stay out of debt would work to our disadvantage, we acted on it anyway.

When we first made that decision, Kenneth and I could not see how we could ever pay cash for a car, much less a home! But we committed to that word anyway. That's what comes from seeking first God's kingdom and exalting His wisdom above all else! What a tremendous blessing it has been.

Ken and I have experienced increase because we had determined to listen to wisdom. That's exactly what the Scripture promises: **Blessed (happy, fortunate, to be envied) is the man who listens to me, watching daily at my gates, waiting at the posts of my doors** (Proverbs 8:34, AMP).

This verse is talking about the person who runs his daily life by the wisdom of God, expecting to hear from Him and paying attention to Him when He speaks. The person who does this is the one who will find wisdom **and obtain favor from the Lord** (v. 35, AMP).

So if you want to obtain the favor of the Lord and establish a strong foundation for prosperity in your life, go after wisdom. As you develop a lifestyle based on the principles of God's Word, you'll begin to experience increase in every area of your life.

I [wisdom] lead in the way of righteousness, in the midst of the paths of judgment: That I may cause those that love me to inherit substance; and I will fill their treasures (Proverbs 8:20-21).

Wisdom for Today

Make the quality decision that whatever God tells you to do, you will do, whether your flesh wants to or not.

Make sure your priorities are right. Strive after wisdom, not material gain.

Put yourself in a position for increase by seeking first God's kingdom and His way of doing and being right.

CHAPTER 9
Be Wise — Be Teachable

*If you are going to grow in God and walk in His
wisdom, you will have to stay teachable — willing to
receive correction without taking offense.*

Proverbs Chapter 9

1   Wisdom hath builded her house, she hath hewn out her seven pillars:

2   She hath killed her beasts; she hath mingled her wine; she hath also furnished her table.

3   She hath sent forth her maidens: she crieth upon the highest places of the city,

4   Whoso is simple, let him turn in hither: as for him that wanteth understanding, she saith to him,

5   Come, eat of my bread, and drink of the wine which I have mingled.

6   Forsake the foolish, and live; and go in the way of understanding.

7   He that reproveth a scorner getteth to himself shame: and he that rebuketh a wicked man getteth himself a blot.

8   Reprove not a scorner, lest he hate thee: rebuke a wise man, and he will love thee.

9   Give instruction to a wise man, and he will be yet wiser: teach a just man, and he will increase in learning.

10   The fear of the Lord is the beginning of wisdom: and the knowledge of the holy is understanding.

11   For by me thy days shall be multiplied, and the years of thy life shall be increased.

12   If thou be wise, thou shalt be wise for thyself: but if thou scornest, thou alone shalt bear it.

13   A foolish woman is clamorous: she is simple, and knoweth nothing.

14   For she sitteth at the door of her house, on a seat in the high places of the city,

15   To call passengers who go right on their ways:

16   Whoso is simple, let him turn in hither: and as for him that wanteth understanding, she saith to him,

17   Stolen waters are sweet, and bread eaten in secret is pleasant.

18   But he knoweth not that the dead are there; and that her guests are in the depths of hell.

Hidden Treasures

✦❁✦

Chapter 9 provides another vital key to walking in the wisdom of God: the ability to take correction. As we look at this chapter, we're going to focus on the subject of being teachable.

This chapter starts out with wisdom once more inviting those who lack understanding to **[forsake the foolish and simpleminded] and live! And walk in the way of insight and understanding** (Proverbs 9:6, AMP). Notice that wisdom always seems to be crying aloud, endeavoring to bring the hardhearted and the naive to their senses so they don't continue on their way to their own destruction.

That speaks of the heart of God. He wants us to walk on His path that leads to abundant life.

Be Willing To Take Correction

✦❁✦

But for God to teach us, we have to be willing to be taught. So after wisdom's invitation comes the divine warning, "Don't be unteachable" (vv. 7-9).

This passage contrasts the way that the scorner and the wise man take correction: **Reprove not a scorner, lest he hate you; reprove a wise man, and he will love you. Give instruction to a wise man and he will be yet wiser** (vv. 8-9, AMP).

A wise man when he is corrected will increase in learning. On the other hand, when a scorner is corrected, everyone better watch out: **He who rebukes a scorner heaps upon himself abuse, and he who reproves a wicked man gets for himself bruises** (v. 7, AMP).

So don't let yourself become a hardhearted scorner of the things of God. Proverbs 15:32 (AMP) says, **He who refuses and ignores instruction and correction despises himself, but he who heeds reproof gets understanding.** Be willing to take correction.

If you sense in your spirit that the Lord is telling you to do or to stop doing something, don't hesitate to receive His correction and change. And don't get offended at Him just because He has asked you to do something you don't want to do. Realize that the Holy Spirit is endeavoring to instruct you for your good. Maybe He's instructing you to avert a trial or temptation that may be farther down your path in life.

The Holy Spirit may say to you, "Drop that habit" or "Don't spend your time doing that activity." What you're doing may not even seem harmful to you at this point in your life. But God may know that your pursuit of that particular course will eventually lead you to a trial or crisis that can be averted — *if* you will listen to Him now.

So don't be offended by the Holy Spirit's correction — be teachable. He lives inside of you to help you. He is telling you what to do because He loves you and wants the best for you.

Graciously Receive Correction From Others

The same thing is true when it comes to receiving correction from others. When you hear something preached from the pulpit that corrects sin in your life, you should never take offense. If what is being said is in the Word of God, just make the adjustment. Do what the Word says. Receive correction.

For example, don't get angry with the preacher in the pulpit if he begins to preach about giving and tithing.

People who are faithful in their tithing and giving don't get angry when the preacher talks about this subject. It makes them feel good that they are honoring God with their finances. But those who aren't giving and tithing the way they should sometimes get a little huffy when the preacher "steps on their toes."

Don't be one of those "huffy" ones. Receive correction and be thankful for it. It is a blessing to be corrected by the Lord.

I know that isn't always easy. In the natural, we don't always like to be corrected. But we just have to make the decision, "I'm going to remain teachable, no matter what anyone says to correct me."

Appreciate those who share the wisdom of God with you. Perhaps someone begins to share something with you from the Word or from their own experience, pointing out an area in your life where you may have missed it. Instead of getting upset, just examine yourself and ask, "Is what this person told me right? Does it agree with the Word? Do I need to make a change here?" Be correctable.

Now, I know that someone might try to correct you in the wrong spirit. But even if the person correcting you does it wrong, don't become offended and try to retaliate. Just tell him that you appreciate him for trying to help you. And if what he says isn't right — if it doesn't agree with the Word — just forget it.

What I'm saying to you is this: Maintain a teachable spirit, and refuse to become offended when you are corrected.

Someone said, "If you think you have already arrived, you aren't going anywhere." That's true.

The truth is, if you are going to grow in God, you may as well get used to those times of correction because they are something you will have to go through. You see, you don't know it all yet. I don't know it all yet. And if we aren't teachable, we will never go further in our walk with God than we are right now.

The Foolish Woman
Versus the Godly Wife

I want to look for a moment now at a scriptural description of a foolish woman: **The foolish woman is noisy; she is simple and open to all forms of evil; she [willfully and recklessly] knows nothing whatever [of eternal value]** (Proverbs 9:13, AMP).

Now let's contrast that description with what the New Testament says about the godly wife, who possesses **the inward adorning and beauty of the hidden person of the heart, with the incorruptible and unfading charm of a gentle and peaceful spirit, which [is not anxious or wrought up, but] is very precious in the sight of God** (1 Peter 3:4, AMP).

So — which kind of woman appeals to you more? Which kind of person would *you* rather be? Good choice! Nobody wants to be a loud, bossy woman.

You know, it's up to you what kind of person you are. You can be proud, stiff-necked and unteachable — or you can be humble, full of peace and loveliness and a blessing to all with whom you come in contact.

Wisdom for Today

*If the Holy Spirit corrects you about something today, don't be offended
— be teachable and change!*

*Make the decision, "I'm going to remain teachable,
no matter what anyone says to correct me."*

*When someone says something to correct you, ask yourself: "Does what this
person said agree with the Word? Do I need to make a change here?"*

Chapter 10
How You Live Makes the Difference

*How we choose to live — in God's wisdom or in the
ways of the world — makes all the difference in
determining the outcome of our lives.*

Proverbs Chapter 10

1   The proverbs of Solomon. A wise son maketh a glad father: but a foolish son is the heaviness of his mother.

2   Treasures of wickedness profit nothing: but righteousness delivereth from death.

3   The Lord will not suffer the soul of the righteous to famish: but he casteth away the substance of the wicked.

4   He becometh poor that dealeth with a slack hand: but the hand of the diligent maketh rich.

5   He that gathereth in summer is a wise son: but he that sleepeth in harvest is a son that causeth shame.

6   Blessings are upon the head of the just: but violence covereth the mouth of the wicked.

7   The memory of the just is blessed: but the name of the wicked shall rot.

8   The wise in heart will receive commandments: but a prating fool shall fall.

9   He that walketh uprightly walketh surely: but he that perverteth his ways shall be known.

10   He that winketh with the eye causeth sorrow: but a prating fool shall fall.

11   The mouth of a righteous man is a well of life: but violence covereth the mouth of the wicked.

12   Hatred stirreth up strifes: but love covereth all sins.

13   In the lips of him that hath understanding wisdom is found: but a rod is for the back of him that is void of understanding.

14   Wise men lay up knowledge: but the mouth of the foolish is near destruction.

15   The rich man's wealth is his strong city: the destruction of the poor is their poverty.

16   The labour of the righteous tendeth to life: the fruit of the wicked to sin.

17   He is in the way of life that keepeth instruction: but he that refuseth reproof erreth.

18   He that hideth hatred with lying lips, and he that uttereth a slander, is a fool.

19   In the multitude of words there wanteth not sin: but he that refraineth his lips is wise.

20   The tongue of the just is as choice silver: the heart of the wicked is little worth.

21   The lips of the righteous feed many: but fools die for want of wisdom.

22 The blessing of the Lord, it maketh rich, and he addeth no sorrow with it.

23 It is as sport to a fool to do mischief: but a man of understanding hath wisdom.

24 The fear of the wicked, it shall come upon him: but the desire of the righteous shall be granted.

25 As the whirlwind passeth, so is the wicked no more: but the righteous is an everlasting foundation.

26 As vinegar to the teeth, and as smoke to the eyes, so is the sluggard to them that send him.

27 The fear of the Lord prolongeth days: but the years of the wicked shall be shortened.

28 The hope of the righteous shall be gladness: but the expectation of the wicked shall perish.

29 The way of the Lord is strength to the upright: but destruction shall be to the workers of iniquity.

30 The righteous shall never be removed: but the wicked shall not inhabit the earth.

31 The mouth of the just bringeth forth wisdom: but the froward tongue shall be cut out.

32 The lips of the righteous know what is acceptable: but the mouth of the wicked speaketh frowardness.

Hidden Treasures

In Proverbs 10, the type and expression of writing changes. The proverbs aren't so tied together; instead, they are more like short little nuggets of divine wisdom.

With that in mind, we're going to go through the rest of Proverbs emphasizing certain verses and themes. Some verses we'll skip over, and others we'll stop for a while to dig into their hidden treasures of wisdom and instruction.

The Righteous Leave a Good Report

A certain statement sticks in my mind as I read through Proverbs 10 and Proverbs 11: *It makes all the difference in the world how you live.*

The law of sowing and reaping is made very evident in these two chapters. Over and over again, the reward of the righteous is contrasted to the ultimate punishment of the wicked.

For example, look at this sharp contrast between the righteous and the wicked: **The memory of the [uncompromisingly] righteous is a blessing, but the name of the wicked shall rot** (Proverbs 10:7, AMP).

You know, if I leave the earth before Jesus comes, I don't want people to be glad when I'm gone. I don't want my family and friends to say, "I am so glad to get her out of here!" Even though they would never say that out loud, I don't want them to be inwardly relieved that I'm gone.

No, I want to be a blessing to people while I live on this earth — and so do you!

And I guarantee you, you *will* be a blessing to others if you fit the description of the righteous in this chapter. For example, your mouth should be a well of life (v. 11). Your love should cover a multitude of transgressions (v. 12, AMP). And wisdom should be found on your lips that feeds and guides many (vv. 13, 21, AMP).

Make no mistake about it: How you live *does* make a difference.

Changing Your Image
From Poverty to Prosperity

Verse 15 (AMP) makes an interesting observation that I want to explore a little bit. It says, **The rich man's wealth is his strong city; the poverty of the poor is their ruin.**

If you have been around very long, you have seen the truth of that statement. People who are wealthy sometimes lose their money through various circumstances. But if you just watch them, you'll find that most of them eventually gain it back — especially if they have been rich most of their lives.

The reason for that is the wealthy *expect* to be rich. Because they made that money once, they just assume they can do it again.

Even if certain wealthy people were born into a family that had money and they didn't do a thing to earn it, they still tend to think in terms of always having plenty, even when hard times come. That's what this scripture is talking about when it says, **The rich man's wealth is his strong city.**

On the other hand, so often those who are in poverty seem to stay there. The majority of people raised in the ghetto live there all their lives. They never get out. It's like a prison, even though there are no walls.

The rich man, whose wealth is his strong city, is accustomed to that wealth, and he doesn't expect to live without it. He can't see himself without it.

But the poor man, who was raised in poverty, has never known anything but lack. Poverty looms up before him like an impenetrable wall, and he just can't see himself climbing over it.

The rich man can't see himself without bread on his table; the poor man can't see himself living in abundance. (Of course, in both cases there are exceptions to the rule.)

But you can go into the ghetto and preach the Word of God to the poor. You can share the truth about the blessings and the love of God, and those who are spiritually hungry want to receive God's truth. And if the poor receive the Word in faith, they can begin to change their poverty into prosperity. The Word works when activated by faith whether a person lives in the slums or in the best neighborhoods of Beverly Hills!

What happens when the poor man hears the Word of God? It changes his image — the picture he sees of himself. It changes that inner picture of poverty that has always loomed before him. Instead, he begins to see himself with his needs met as God promised in His Word.

If *you've* been living with a poverty mentality, you need to change your image of yourself in the area of finances. So start seeing yourself with your needs met. Dare to see yourself as God declares you in His Word. Act on His Word and be faithful to give into God's kingdom. Each day *expect* Him to bring you increase. Then just watch what He will do to cause you to prosper in Him!

Walk in the Counsel of the Godly

There are times in life when we may need to seek the counsel of another to find a solution to our problem. And of course, we all need times of fellowship with each other.

Make sure you heed these divine instructions when seeking counsel or friendship: **The tongues of those who are upright and in right standing with God are as choice silver; the minds of those who are wicked and out of harmony with God are of little value** (Proverbs 10:20, AMP).

That certainly is the truth! In other words, don't go to those who are out of harmony with God; go to the godly. The counsel of the righteous is as choice silver, but the counsel of the wicked is worthless.

The Bible says you're blessed when you seek out godly counsel: **Blessed (Happy, fortunate, prosperous, and enviable) is the man who walks and lives not in the counsel of the ungodly [following their advice, their plans and purposes]...nor sits down [to relax and rest] where the scornful [and the mockers] gather** (Psalm 1:1, AMP).

Blessed is the man who doesn't spend his time with the ungodly. He knows that close association with such people only adds to his challenge of walking uprightly before the Lord.

Here we see that the kind of people you fellowship with also makes a difference in determining the outcome of your life. You see, the ungodly will pull you in another direction. You should be keeping company with those who love God and are pure in heart.

The best thing you can do is to find people who love God more than you do and keep company with them. You'll put yourself in a position to grow spiritually as their godly influence pulls you up to their level.

On the other hand, if you spend time with ungodly people, they will continually pull you down. That's why it's so important to fellowship with **those who are upright and in right standing with God** (Proverbs 10:20, AMP).

What happens to the person who walks not in the counsel of the ungodly but in the counsel of God? **He shall be like a tree firmly planted [and tended] by the streams of water, ready to bring forth its fruit in its season; its leaf also shall not fade or wither; and everything he does shall prosper [and come to maturity]** (Psalm 1:3, AMP).

That is the prosperous life that God intends for us to live! But it all depends on how we decide to live.

Long Life or Days Cut Short?

For the most part, *how* we live can also determine *how long* we live.

We've already seen that walking in wisdom brings length of days and a life worth living (Proverbs 3:2, AMP). But sin can cut your life short: **The reverent and worshipful fear of the Lord prolongs one's days, but the years of the wicked shall be made short** (Proverbs 10:27, AMP).

It isn't God's will for you to die young. He wants you to live out the full number of your days: **With *long life* will I satisfy him, and show him my**

salvation (Psalm 91:16). This promise is given to the person who abides in Him (Psalm 91:1).

On the basis of this scripture, if you live seventy or eighty years and still aren't satisfied, just keep on living until you are! (Feel free to live 120 years if you aren't satisfied.)

That's what the patriarchs of old did. They lived until they were ready to go home. Then when they were old, plenteous in goods and satisfied with their life, God just "gathered them unto their people" (Genesis 25:8). In other words, they were gathered to their family that was already on the other side.

Did you know heaven is a real place? You have family waiting for you there. And the older you become, the more family members will gather there before you.

The Bible says that to be absent from the body is to be present with the Lord (2 Corinthians 5:8). It also says that to be present with the Lord in heaven is *far* better (Philippians 1:23).

So when you leave this earth, you will instantly be with the Lord. And you will also be "gathered unto your people."

The first people you will see in heaven will be your family members. Even members you have never met before will come out to greet you. It will be a grand reunion!

Also, anyone whom you helped lead to the Lord while on earth will be there to greet you. So the more souls you bring into God's kingdom during this life, the bigger your reception will be when you go to be with the Lord.

Heaven is a real place, and it will be glorious someday to be gathered to our people in the presence of the Lord. Yet even though we are citizens of heaven, we should want to live out our lives on this earth so we can fulfill what we are called to do. We must run the race that has been set before us and finish our course (Hebrews 12:1). Meanwhile, we can enjoy all the rights and privileges that our heavenly citizenship provides for us now in this life.

Perhaps you haven't been living according to God's wisdom. You may have even been living in a manner that has destined you to die young.

Well, you can change that destiny. You can come over to God's side right now and make Jesus Lord of your life. You can begin to walk in His wisdom and His ways. He won't hold your past against you. He'll just wipe away all your past mistakes and give you the blessings that belong to you as a new creation in Christ Jesus — including long life!

It's your choice. If you choose to live the world's way, you will very likely cut your days short, and the days that you do live won't be worth living. But if you choose to walk with God, you can enjoy a long, satisfying life full of good days — with far better days yet to come in heaven.

God is making it very clear — how you live does make the difference!

Wisdom for Today

*Ask God every day to make you a blessing
to people while you live on this earth.*

*Live each day expecting God to bring you increase
as you are faithful to give into His kingdom.*

When you need counsel and fellowship, go to the godly.

CHAPTER 11
The Recompense of the Righteous

*Those who sow righteousness and walk in God's
wisdom will reap a great recompense of reward both on
this earth and throughout eternity.*

❦

Proverbs Chapter 11

1 A false balance is abomination to the Lord: but a just weight is his delight.

2 When pride cometh, then cometh shame: but with the lowly is wisdom.

3 The integrity of the upright shall guide them: but the perverseness of transgressors shall destroy them.

4 Riches profit not in the day of wrath: but righteousness delivereth from death.

5 The righteousness of the perfect shall direct his way: but the wicked shall fall by his own wickedness.

6 The righteousness of the upright shall deliver them: but transgressors shall be taken in their own naughtiness.

7 When a wicked man dieth, his expectation shall perish: and the hope of unjust men perisheth.

8 The righteous is delivered out of trouble, and the wicked cometh in his stead.

9 An hypocrite with his mouth destroyeth his neighbour: but through knowledge shall the just be delivered.

10 When it goeth well with the righteous, the city rejoiceth: and when the wicked perish, there is shouting.

11 By the blessing of the upright the city is exalted: but it is overthrown by the mouth of the wicked.

12 He that is void of wisdom despiseth his neighbour: but a man of understanding holdeth his peace.

13 A talebearer revealeth secrets: but he that is of a faithful spirit concealeth the matter.

14 Where no counsel is, the people fall: but in the multitude of counsellors there is safety.

15 He that is surety for a stranger shall smart for it: and he that hateth suretiship is sure.

16 A gracious woman retaineth honour: and strong men retain riches.

17 The merciful man doeth good to his own soul: but he that is cruel troubleth his own flesh.

18 The wicked worketh a deceitful work: but to him that soweth righteousness shall be a sure reward.

19 As righteousness tendeth to life: so he that pursueth evil pursueth it to his own death.

20 They that are of a froward heart are abomination to the Lord: but such as are upright in their way are his delight.

21 Though hand join in hand, the wicked shall not be unpunished: but the seed of the righteous shall be delivered.

22 As a jewel of gold in a swine's snout, so is a fair woman which is without discretion.

23 The desire of the righteous is only good: but the expectation of the wicked is wrath.

24 There is that scattereth, and yet increaseth; and there is that withholdeth more than is meet, but it tendeth to poverty.

25 The liberal soul shall be made fat: and he that watereth shall be watered also himself.

26 He that withholdeth corn, the people shall curse him: but blessing shall be upon the head of him that selleth it.

27 He that diligently seeketh good procureth favour: but he that seeketh mischief, it shall come unto him.

28 He that trusteth in his riches shall fall: but the righteous shall flourish as a branch.

29 He that troubleth his own house shall inherit the wind: and the fool shall be servant to the wise of heart.

30 The fruit of the righteous is a tree of life; and he that winneth souls is wise.

31 Behold, the righteous shall be recompensed in the earth: much more the wicked and the sinner.

Hidden Treasures

Proverbs 11 gives us many more examples of the law of sowing and reaping at work in the earth. What God says about that law is very blunt and to the point: **Whatever a man sows, that and that only is what he will reap** (Galatians 6:7, AMP).

The thought to remember as we go through this chapter is this: *The righteous have an advantage.* I want you to get that truth into your thinking forever!

Those who go their own wicked way will reap destruction. But those who sow righteousness and walk in His wisdom will find deliverance, direction and increase, for **the [uncompromisingly] righteous shall be recompensed on earth!** (Proverbs 11:31, AMP).

We Haven't Seen Anything Yet!

Ken and I can add our testimony to the truth of that verse. God has certainly recompensed us for our obedience to His Word. We have prospered for many years, and we continue to increase.

And we're going to keep increasing, because we are continuing to sow the Word of God into our hearts and to do as we are told. And we're determined to keep following God's way of doing and being right. The more we know of God's wisdom, the more accurately we can walk before the Lord. And the more accurately we walk, the more of the blessing of God is manifested in our lives.

You see, our prosperity in God as believers is the result of living a lifestyle of godly principles one day after the next, month after month, year after year. The more we sow the Word into our hearts and walk out the wisdom of God in our lives, the more we're going to increase. There is just no end to it. We'll keep increasing from now on throughout eternity.

And we haven't seen anything yet. None of us have seen anything compared to the recompense God has for His people in the earth before Jesus returns. Talk about increase! We're going to see increase within the Body of Christ like we've never imagined. One area of increase will be the transfer of the wealth from the wicked into the hands of the just. That must happen before the end of this age (Proverbs 13:22).

As we witness the recompense of the righteous in the last days, we will think, *This is so wonderful. This is so big. This is so great!* Then Jesus will come and we'll be caught away with Him in the air (1 Thessalonians 4:17).

That's when we'll see what increase is really all about! In heaven we'll find out that we just barely started experiencing increase while we lived on the earth.

Sow Righteousness, Reap Rewards

So let's just look at a few of the verses in Proverbs 11 that show the law of sowing and reaping at work to recompense the righteous in this life.

First, those who walk in wisdom and righteousness can expect divine guidance and direction: **The integrity of the upright shall guide them, but the willful contrariness and crookedness of the treacherous shall destroy them** (Proverbs 11:3, AMP).

The righteous also have God's promise of deliverance: **The [uncompromisingly] righteous is delivered out of trouble, and the wicked gets into it instead** (v. 8, AMP).

Then God promises that a person's righteous deeds of love and mercy will return to him as a harvest of blessing: **The merciful, kind and generous man** benefits himself [for his deeds return to bless him], but he who is cruel and callous [to the wants of others] brings on himself retribution (v. 17, AMP).

Jesus gave us a similar promise of recompense: **Be merciful (sympathetic, tender, responsive, and compassionate) even as your Father is [all these].... Give, and [gifts] will be given to you; good measure, pressed down, shaken together, and running over** (Luke 6:36, 38, AMP).

In other words, every time you are merciful, kind or generous to someone else, you are blessing yourself because your loving deeds will return to bless you. You are sowing righteousness, so you will enjoy a sure reward (Proverbs 11:18).

On the other hand, a person who sows cruelty and callousness in his dealings with others will reap retribution in his relationships and in his life. And God doesn't have to do a thing — the cruel and callous person has done it to himself. He opened the door to the devil and put himself under the curse of the law.

Don't Be a Talebearer — Keep the Matter Hidden

One of the greatest acts of kindness and faithfulness you can sow into someone's life is to keep his confidences: **He who goes about as a talebearer reveals secrets, but he who is trustworthy and faithful in spirit** *keeps the matter hidden* (v. 13, AMP).

I once found an interesting definition in a concordance for the Greek word *diabolos* that fits in with this verse. For one thing, *diabolos* means *devil.* But it also means *one who falsely accuses and divides people without cause.*

The devil is an accuser and a slanderer, called by that name because originally he accused and slandered God in the Garden of Eden. The serpent told Eve, "Do you know why God doesn't want you to eat of that fruit, Eve? He doesn't want you to be as smart as He is!" (Genesis 3:4-5, author's paraphrase). (Think about it. Satan continually accuses God to you: "God doesn't care." "God isn't going to answer your prayers." "God's going to let you stay sick." The devil wants to talk you out of believing what God says. He and his evil spirits try to get you to doubt God. Don't listen to unbelief — rebuke it in Jesus' name.)

So when talebearers accuse and slander others with the gossip and lies they spread, they are acting like the original accuser!

The devil likes to use a talebearer to pass on diabolical information about someone to others. Satan is *diabolos*, the one who falsely accuses and divides people without any reason. He knows that people who are divided from one another are not loving, open and kind to each other and division gives him entrance.

So if you're spending time listening to someone who is a talebearer and a gossip, you are partaking of the wrong company! **He who goes about as a talebearer reveals secrets; therefore associate not with him who talks too freely** (Proverbs 20:19, AMP).

People who like to reveal others' secrets can cause a great deal of strife among the people with whom they associate. Many times the tales they pass on may even be true but certainly not pure, lovely or good reports (Philippians 4:8). Whether they are true or not, gossiping about them causes strife.

We saw that one of the things God hates most is for someone to sow discord among the brethren (Proverbs 6:19). I'm telling you, you want to stay clear of a talebearer who accuses others and spreads strife. And you definitely want to make sure you aren't that kind of person yourself!

So just keep sowing mercy, kindness and righteousness. Keep doing what is right before God. And as you stay steadfast in righteousness, you will attain to life (Proverbs 11:19, AMP). As you are blameless in your ways, you will be His delight (v. 20, AMP). You will flourish as a green bough, and the fruit of your righteousness will be as a tree of life to you (vv. 28, 30, AMP).

Have you made the decision to walk in the ways of wisdom? When you do, all of these divine promises and many, many more are your recompense to claim both on this earth and in the ages to come!

Wisdom for Today

*Be merciful, kind and generous to someone else —
and bless yourself in the process!*

*If someone tells you something in confidence,
be faithful to keep the matter hidden.*

*Don't partake of the wrong company. If someone talks
too freely about others, steer clear of him!*

CHAPTER 12
Dealing Wisely in the Affairs of Life

You must have diligence and faith to deal wisely
in the affairs of daily life. So diligently plant God's
Word in your heart, and then speak it forth by faith
into your circumstances!

Proverbs Chapter 12

1   Whoso loveth instruction loveth knowledge: but he that hateth reproof is brutish.

2   A good man obtaineth favour of the Lord: but a man of wicked devices will he condemn.

3   A man shall not be established by wickedness: but the root of the righteous shall not be moved.

4   A virtuous woman is a crown to her husband: but she that maketh ashamed is as rottenness in his bones.

5   The thoughts of the righteous are right: but the counsels of the wicked are deceit.

6   The words of the wicked are to lie in wait for blood: but the mouth of the upright shall deliver them.

7   The wicked are overthrown, and are not: but the house of the righteous shall stand.

8   A man shall be commended according to his wisdom: but he that is of a perverse heart shall be despised.

9   He that is despised, and hath a servant, is better than he that honoureth himself, and lacketh bread.

10   A righteous man regardeth the life of his beast: but the tender mercies of the wicked are cruel.

11   He that tilleth his land shall be satisfied with bread: but he that followeth vain persons is void of understanding.

12   The wicked desireth the net of evil men: but the root of the righteous yieldeth fruit.

13   The wicked is snared by the transgression of his lips: but the just shall come out of trouble.

14   A man shall be satisfied with good by the fruit of his mouth: and the recompence of a man's hands shall be rendered unto him.

15   The way of a fool is right in his own eyes: but he that hearkeneth unto counsel is wise.

16   A fool's wrath is presently known: but a prudent man covereth shame.

17   He that speaketh truth showeth forth righteousness: but a false witness deceit.

18   There is that speaketh like the piercings of a sword: but the tongue of the wise is health.

19   The lip of truth shall be established for ever: but a lying tongue is but for a moment.

20   Deceit is in the heart of them that imagine evil: but to the counsellors of peace is joy.

21 There shall no evil happen to the just: but the wicked shall be filled with mischief.

22 Lying lips are abomination to the Lord: but they that deal truly are his delight.

23 A prudent man concealeth knowledge: but the heart of fools proclaimeth foolishness.

24 The hand of the diligent shall bear rule: but the slothful shall be under tribute.

25 Heaviness in the heart of man maketh it stoop: but a good word maketh it glad.

26 The righteous is more excellent than his neighbour: but the way of the wicked seduceth them.

27 The slothful man roasteth not that which he took in hunting: but the substance of a diligent man is precious.

28 In the way of righteousness is life; and in the pathway thereof there is no death.

Hidden Treasures

One of the themes emphasized in Proverbs 12 is how to deal wisely in the affairs of life. Although there are many important spiritual principles in this chapter we could discuss, we're going to focus on just two of them.

God's Word — Supernatural Seed

Our words are vital in determining how we deal with the affairs of life. There are two verses in this chapter referring to the power of words that I want to talk about.

First, verse 6 says, **The mouth of the upright shall deliver them.** Then verse 14 states, **A man shall be satisfied with good by the fruit of his mouth.**

We've already seen that we are to keep God's Word in our mouth (Joshua 1:8). But how can the fruit of our mouth effect deliverance in our lives and satisfy us with good things?

God gives us the answer to that question: **For as the rain and snow come down from the heavens, and return not there again, but water the earth and make it bring forth and sprout... So shall My word be that goes forth out of My mouth** (Isaiah 55:10-11, AMP).

Just as the rain comes down from heaven, soaks into the earth and makes it bring forth and bud, *so shall God's Word be:* **It shall not return to Me** void [without producing any effect, useless], but it shall accomplish that which I please and purpose, and it shall prosper in the thing for which I sent it (Isaiah 55:11, AMP).

God's Word has the power within itself to accomplish that for which it is sent.

The Word comes down from heaven. It's quick. It's alive. It's energized and full of power (Hebrews 4:12, AMP). It goes into the ground of our heart and brings forth its God-ordained harvest.

You see, the seed of the Word is made to be planted in the soil of our hearts. We can find further insight into that truth in the Mark 4 account of the sower who sowed the Word.

Jesus explained to His disciples that the Word is the seed, and the heart of man is the ground. Jesus went on to explain some of the things that will keep the Word from producing in a person's heart.

In order to produce the harvest God intends, the Word has to be received and taken into your heart. It has to be guarded and kept in the midst of your heart during trouble and persecution. Your heart can't be overcrowded with the cares of this world and the lusts of other things for the Word seed to produce (Mark 4:16-19).

In Jesus' explanation of this parable, He made an interesting point. He said that some people just won't be able to bring forth a crop because of the condition of the soil in their hearts. When the seed is sown in hearts likened to a hardened path, stony ground or a thorn patch, the poor condition of the soil causes the seed to either wither away or be made fruitless.

You see, it's never the Word's fault. The Word always produces. Just like natural seed, the Word has the power hidden within it to reproduce itself. As one minister said, "The Word is like natural seed. Everything depends on the treatment it gets."

Genesis 1:11 mentions this quality about seed. And although this verse is talking about natural seed, the same thing holds true for the supernatural seed of the Word: **And God said, Let the earth bring forth grass, the herb yielding seed, and the fruit tree yielding fruit after his kind, *whose seed is in itself*, upon the earth.**

You know, I have poppies in my yard that bloom in the spring and begin to dry up in the heat of the summer. When the petals all fall off, it's easy to see that the center of just one of those little poppies holds a multitude of tiny, little seeds.

But what is amazing to me is that within each one of those little seeds lies an entire poppy plant!

That's just the way a seed works. The seed has the power within it to reproduce itself.

So God compares natural seed to the seed of the Word, saying, **So shall My word be that goes forth out of My mouth** (Isaiah 55:11, AMP).

In other words, within God's Word is His creative power to bring His promise to pass.

Thank God, we have His wisdom and His Word written down for us so that we can be as full of that supernatural seed as we want to be. We may be limited in how much money we can deposit in our bank account. But if we have a Bible, we are *not* limited in how much Word we can deposit in our hearts!

God has given us scriptures of blessing and promise — supernatural seed to be planted in the good soil of our hearts and then spoken out of our mouths in faith. Faith released in the spiritual realm brings tangible substance in the natural realm (Hebrews 11:1).

You see, God created the world out of nothing we can see. He did it with His words. He spoke words of faith, and those words created everything we see around us.

Now we are to speak forth the Word abiding in our hearts. As we do, we will bring forth substance — wisdom, healing, provision or deliverance — from the spirit realm into this natural realm. We will be satisfied with good by the fruit of our mouth (Proverbs 12:14).

As we speak God's wisdom and power into our daily affairs our lives will be transformed.

That's how the mouth of the upright delivers them!

The Reward of Diligence

Diligence is another key to dealing wisely in the affairs of life: **The hand of the diligent will rule, but the slothful will be put to forced labor** (v. 24, AMP). God has much to say about diligence. It takes diligence in the spiritual and in the natural realm to increase, according to God's Word. I think it is safe to say that you won't go far without diligence.

If you want to be victorious, be diligent. If you want to be defeated, be slothful.

The Bible also says that **the diligent man gets precious possessions** (v. 27, AMP). There is great reward in being diligent. The provision and the power of God will work on your behalf when you are diligently living in pursuit of God and His Word and His plan for your life.

To be diligent means *to make an intense effort or to exert oneself intensely; to be steady in application to business and constant in effort or exertion to accomplish what is undertaken.* It means *to be attentive and industrious, not idle or negligent.*

Diligence is a steady application to business of any kind. For example, whether you're a boss or an employee, you should apply yourself faithfully to the success of your business or job.

Let's look at a few other verses in Proverbs that talk about being diligent. Proverbs 10:4 says, **The hand of the diligent maketh rich.** Then Proverbs 13:4 in the *New International Version* tells us that **the desires of the diligent are fully satisfied.**

Diligence is the opposite of being lazy, and as I heard one minister say, "God doesn't bless lazy Christians." There is a lot of truth to that statement.

So don't expect to be lazy and still prosper and increase. Increase comes as you make the effort to apply God's spiritual principles to your life. As you are diligent to do that, you have so much more advantage in your life compared to someone who just lives from day to day without any thought of God. You become elevated from being *controlled* by your circumstances to being *in control* of them.

For instance, walking in God's principles will transform your attitude about your job, even if it's a job you don't like. You'll be set free from bondage to a job, into the freedom of enjoying any job. Instead of just trying to make it through your workshift, you'll live each day in victory, confident that your future is in God's hands and that He will promote you as you are diligent to obey Him.

Above all else, diligence is necessary to increase in the things of God. You can't just tap into the laws of the spirit in a careless manner.

In order to have the knowledge of God imparted to your heart, a process of diligence is required. God doesn't just dump the wisdom and understanding of His higher ways on you. You have to seek them by spending time in His Word and in prayer.

The Scripture says when we seek God, we will find Him (Matthew 7:7). The word *seek* implies an intense effort.

For instance, if you were seeking a job, you wouldn't just sit at home and watch television, waiting for someone to come to you. You'd go out into the marketplace, knocking on doors and making appointments for job interviews.

That's the kind of continual effort we need to employ when seeking God. We have to be diligent in the things of God, constant in our effort to learn of His ways and to walk in them. And as we diligently pursue God's wisdom and plant an abundance of His Word in our hearts, we will become experts at dealing wisely in the affairs of life!

Wisdom for Today

Make sure the soil of your heart is good ground for God's supernatural seed, then continually plant that seed in your heart.

Speak forth in faith the Word planted in your heart, and bring forth the harvest you need.

Be diligent in the things of God, constant in your effort to walk closer to Him.

CHAPTER 13
The Law of Gradual Increase

As you walk with God and obey His Word,
the law of increase begins to operate — little by little,
in every realm of life.

⁂

Proverbs Chapter 13

1 A wise son heareth his father's instruction: but a scorner heareth not rebuke.

2 A man shall eat good by the fruit of his mouth: but the soul of the transgressors shall eat violence.

3 He that keepeth his mouth keepeth his life: but he that openeth wide his lips shall have destruction.

4 The soul of the sluggard desireth, and hath nothing: but the soul of the diligent shall be made fat.

5 A righteous man hateth lying: but a wicked man is loathsome, and cometh to shame.

6 Righteousness keepeth him that is upright in the way: but wickedness overthroweth the sinner.

7 There is that maketh himself rich, yet hath nothing: there is that maketh himself poor, yet hath great riches.

8 The ransom of a man's life are his riches: but the poor heareth not rebuke.

9 The light of the righteous rejoiceth: but the lamp of the wicked shall be put out.

10 Only by pride cometh contention: but with the well advised is wisdom.

11 Wealth gotten by vanity shall be diminished: but he that gathereth by labour shall increase.

12 Hope deferred maketh the heart sick: but when the desire cometh, it is a tree of life.

13 Whoso despiseth the word shall be destroyed: but he that feareth the commandment shall be rewarded.

14 The law of the wise is a fountain of life, to depart from the snares of death.

15 Good understanding giveth favour: but the way of transgressors is hard.

16 Every prudent man dealeth with knowledge: but a fool layeth open his folly.

17 A wicked messenger falleth into mischief: but a faithful ambassador is health.

18 Poverty and shame shall be to him that refuseth instruction: but he that regardeth reproof shall be honoured.

19 The desire accomplished is sweet to the soul: but it is abomination to fools to depart from evil.

20 He that walketh with wise men shall be wise: but a companion of fools shall be destroyed.

21 Evil pursueth sinners: but to the righteous good shall be repaid.

22 A good man leaveth an inheritance to his children's children: and the wealth of the sinner is laid up for the just.

23 Much food is in the tillage of the poor: but there is that is destroyed for want of judgment.

24 He that spareth his rod hateth his son: but he that loveth him chasteneth him betimes.

25 The righteous eateth to the satisfying of his soul: but the belly of the wicked shall want.

Hidden Treasures

Although there are many things we could discuss in Proverbs 13, I want to explore one particular principle that's very important for success in your walk with God. That principle is found in Proverbs 13:11 (AMP): **Wealth [not earned but] won in haste or unjustly or from the production of things for vain or detrimental use [such riches] will dwindle away, but** *he who gathers little by little will increase* **[his riches].**

This verse is talking about *the spiritual law of gradual increase.* Actually, it is a physical law as well as a spiritual law. A seed planted in the ground doesn't just grow into a plant overnight.

Jesus said that the kingdom of heaven is like a tiny mustard seed that grows into a great tree with birds roosting on its branches (Mark 4:30-32). Well, mustard trees take awhile to grow, and so do the things of God in our heart!

A Personal Testimony of Gradual Increase

From my own experience, I can tell you this: The day Ken and I found out that we could put God's Word to work in our lives and it would bring us success, our lives began to improve immediately, but our finances began to improve gradually. You could say "slowly but surely"!

It usually takes some time to set the blessing laws in motion when you have been operating in the world's system of finances all your life. It shouldn't be as slow for you as it was for us in the late sixties. There is so much more teaching available about God's laws of prosperity now than there was then.

At that time, Ken and I were many thousands of dollars in debt. Ken was thirty years old and a full-time student at Oral Roberts University. He had a family to support and no job.

We were in terrible shape financially and had been that way for a while. Then we learned that God wanted to prosper and bless us. As God's Word was revealed to us we began to act on the Word regarding our finances and to speak God's Word into our situation. We began to tithe first before paying any bills or buying groceries. We began to give into the kingdom of God as the Lord directed. The "seeds" we planted were small, but seeds *were* planted!

Although our financial crop didn't come immediately, we just began to increase little by little. And in about eleven months, we were totally out of debt! It seemed much slower than we wanted, but, after all, it had taken years to create such a financially unsound situation. Looking back now, only eleven months seems an understandable and even a miraculously short time to change a family's entire financial way of operation forever — a permanent change from defeat to victory!

Stay Steady Until the Increase Comes

That's how God normally operates in your life, not only financially but spiritually. You begin to increase in your walk with God a little at a time.

But if you're not careful, the increase won't be fast enough for your satisfaction, and you'll get discouraged. So when your answer seems slow in coming, just let the force of patience rise up within you. Keep on walking with God. Remind yourself that both spiritual and natural blessings are constantly increasing in your life, however slow that increase may seem. The book of Hebrews says through faith and patience we inherit the promises of God (Hebrews 6:12).

Ken and I didn't get out of debt overnight, but we did get out of debt. We didn't purchase a nice home debt free overnight, but one day that dream actually came to pass. We just stayed steady and let the law of increase do its work in our lives.

Increase — An Eternal Reality

And that spiritual law is still operating in our lives. We're still on the increase. And you will be, too, as long as you walk with God and obey His Word!

No matter what your level of faith is in your own spiritual walk, if you stay faithful to God's Word, you will keep increasing. That's the way the blessing of God works.

You'll never reach a point where God says, "I know you are still walking with Me, but that's all the increase you're going to get." As long as you walk with God and believe His Word, you will continue to increase spiritually and financially. You become stronger. You receive more revelation. You understand more about your call and your destiny in God.

Possessing the Inheritance
Little by Little

We can even see the law of gradual increase in the Old Testament. When God sent Israel in to possess the Promised Land, He told them that it was their land. It belonged to them. He had given it into their hands. Yet the Bible says that the Israelites took the land little by little (Exodus 23:30).

That was God's wisdom in operation. The Israelites had a lot of territory to conquer, and they also had to learn a lot about how to cooperate with God. If they had tried to possess all the land too quickly, they would not have been able.

In the same way, God knows that you aren't able to handle His increase in your life all at once — because it includes an increase of responsibility as well as an increase of His blessings. So He takes you up higher in your walk with Him, step by step.

What if Ken and I had received everything we prayed for within the first thirty days of finding out we could believe God for those needs to be met? We might have gotten overwhelmed with it all. But God brought increase into our lives gradually as we knew what to do with it.

If you are faithful over little, then you are able to become ruler over much (Luke 19:17). So you need to determine within yourself not to become discouraged. You have to stay with it, believing God even when the answers seem slow in coming.

Gradual Increase Through Tithing

For example, you don't just try tithing for six weeks and then quit if you aren't president of your company yet! You don't tithe just to be blessed. You give your tithe because it belongs to God and He says it is the right thing to do (Malachi 3:7-10). Your motive is obedience to God's Word to give honor to Him.

You will never increase supernaturally nor grow financially until you tithe. If you don't tithe then, this time next year and even ten years from now, most likely you'll still be digging yourself out of the same old pile of bills and debts. Even if your income increases, your financial situation won't improve. The bills and expenses will increase to keep you in the same financial bondage you've been fighting for years.

But when you begin to honor God with your money, He will begin to honor you with increase. You'll begin to see a difference in your financial situation.

However, tithing in itself isn't the answer to your financial situation; you have to tithe in *faith*. Just paying that first 10 percent with a bad attitude and inward groaning isn't the answer.

First you have to get your motives right. Study the scriptures that pertain to tithing. Find out *why* you're putting your tithe in the offering plate.

Then don't just tithe. Tithe in *faith*. Do it believing that when you tithe, God rebukes the devourer for your sake. Tithe believing God's promise that He will open the windows of heaven and pour out such a blessing that you won't have room to receive it (Malachi 3:10-11). Build your faith in this area with the Word of God and then release faith when you bring the tithe to the Lord. Bring it to Him in worship, thanksgiving and rejoicing (Deuteronomy 26:10-11).

Just keep walking in obedience, honoring God with your finances. Keep tithing in faith and giving offerings. As you do, you will set the law of increase into motion in your life.

Even before the increase ever shows up in your bank account, you will discover that your money seems to go further. Soon you will realize that you're making progress and that the financial pressure has begun to decrease. Keep moving forward. You are putting God's spiritual laws to work in your life. Don't let the devil or circumstances slow you down. God's Word is right, and it will produce what He promises.

The Sinner's Wealth
Laid Up for the Just

❦

Proverbs 13:22 is an exciting scripture that shows us one way God plans to bring increase to the Body of Christ in these last days before the return of Jesus Christ: **The wealth of the sinner is laid up for the just.**

Ecclesiastes 2:26 says something similar: **For God giveth to a man that is good in his sight wisdom, and knowledge, and joy: but to the sinner he giveth travail, to gather and to heap up, that he may give to him that is good before God.**

Sinners actually have the job of storing up wealth for the righteous! You see, the earth is the Lord's to give (Psalm 24:1). So when He promised the land of Canaan to the children of Israel, He didn't mind moving out the ungodly people who lived there, because they weren't the people to whom He had given that land. They weren't His people. They didn't have a covenant with Him. They had not received title deed from Him.

After the heathen were dispossessed, God gave the Promised Land — land that the heathen had already farmed, settled and built houses on — to His covenant people. The wealth of the sinner had been laid up for the just.

And God is in the process of doing the same thing for His Church today! You see, we are in the days of the end-time transfer of wealth about which this verse speaks. Not too long ago, the Lord spoke in my spirit, "It is exceedingly-abundantly-above-all-that-you-can-ask-or-think time!"

I believe Jesus will come in my lifetime. In these last days before His return, we are going to see a greater harvest of souls than we've ever known.

So from now until the end, there will be a great need for money in the Church to do the work of God. Harvest time is the most expensive time. That's why I believe the Lord has begun to perform a transfer of end-time wealth from the world to the Body of Christ. The Church is going to experience greater financial blessing than ever before.

God has ordained a space of time in which we can fulfill His purpose for these last days. We have a big job to do and a short time to do it. God wants to pour money into the hands of His people. But He has to find people whom He can trust to do what He says with that money.

God is teaching us how to withdraw great riches from our heavenly account so we can get the gospel preached to the world and still have plenty left over to enjoy. As we increase our giving, we will see ever-increasing returns. The reservoirs of wicked men will be tapped by the power of God. Some will lose it, and some will come into the kingdom of God themselves and bring their money with them. That's God's best, but either way the wealth of the sinner is laid up for the just!

I'm telling you, it's time to stretch our faith and believe God for our financial inheritance! Increase is the way of God's kingdom. And whether the blessings come quickly or a little at a time, the law of increase will never stop operating in our lives as long as we hold fast to God's ways.

Wisdom for Today

*If the answer to a need seems slow in coming, stay steady.
Remind yourself that the law of gradual increase is
operating in your life and requires patience.*

*Plant seed for a financial harvest: Confess God's Word, be faithful in
tithing and in giving, and expect God to give the increase!*

*When you tithe, release your faith, trusting God to open the windows of
heaven and pour you out a blessing that there is not room enough to receive!*

CHAPTER 14
Keep Your Focus on God's Word

You can walk through any test or trial in supernatural peace and joy. But it's up to you to guard your heart and keep your focus on God and His Word.

❧

Proverbs Chapter 14

1 Every wise woman buildeth her house: but the foolish plucketh it down with her hands.

2 He that walketh in his uprightness feareth the Lord: but he that is perverse in his ways despiseth him.

3 In the mouth of the foolish is a rod of pride: but the lips of the wise shall preserve them.

4 Where no oxen are, the crib is clean: but much increase is by the strength of the ox.

5 A faithful witness will not lie: but a false witness will utter lies.

6 A scorner seeketh wisdom, and findeth it not: but knowledge is easy unto him that understandeth.

7 Go from the presence of a foolish man, when thou perceivest not in him the lips of knowledge.

8 The wisdom of the prudent is to understand his way: but the folly of fools is deceit.

9 Fools make a mock at sin: but among the righteous there is favour.

10 The heart knoweth his own bitterness; and a stranger doth not intermeddle with his joy.

11 The house of the wicked shall be overthrown: but the tabernacle of the upright shall flourish.

12 There is a way which seemeth right unto a man, but the end thereof are the ways of death.

13 Even in laughter the heart is sorrowful; and the end of that mirth is heaviness.

14 The backslider in heart shall be filled with his own ways: and a good man shall be satisfied from himself.

15 The simple believeth every word: but the prudent man looketh well to his going.

16 A wise man feareth, and departeth from evil: but the fool rageth, and is confident.

17 He that is soon angry dealeth foolishly: and a man of wicked devices is hated.

18 The simple inherit folly: but the prudent are crowned with knowledge.

19 The evil bow before the good; and the wicked at the gates of the righteous.

20 The poor is hated even of his own neighbour: but the rich hath many friends.

21 He that despiseth his neighbour sinneth: but he that hath mercy on the poor, happy is he.

22 Do they not err that devise evil? but mercy and truth shall be to them that devise good.

23 In all labour there is profit: but the talk of the lips tendeth only to penury.

24 The crown of the wise is their riches: but the foolishness of fools is folly.

25 A true witness delivereth souls: but a deceitful witness speaketh lies.

26 In the fear of the Lord is strong confidence: and his children shall have a place of refuge.

27 The fear of the Lord is a fountain of life, to depart from the snares of death.

28 In the multitude of people is the king's honour: but in the want of people is the destruction of the prince.

29 He that is slow to wrath is of great understanding: but he that is hasty of spirit exalteth folly.

30 A sound heart is the life of the flesh: but envy the rottenness of the bones.

31 He that oppresseth the poor reproacheth his Maker: but he that honoureth him hath mercy on the poor.

32 The wicked is driven away in his wickedness: but the righteous hath hope in his death.

33 Wisdom resteth in the heart of him that hath understanding: but that which is in the midst of fools is made known.

34 Righteousness exalteth a nation: but sin is a reproach to any people.

35 The king's favour is toward a wise servant: but his wrath is against him that causeth shame.

Hidden Treasures

You can reach a place in your spiritual walk where you are so focused on God's Word that no circumstance can disturb your joy, no trial can shake your peace and no devil can steal your goods. That's the place in God we're going to talk about in our discussion of Proverbs 14.

You Are the Guardian of Your Heart

Keeping your heart is absolutely no one else's responsibility but your own (Proverbs 4:23). No one can guard it but you: **A good man shall be satisfied with [the fruit of] his ways [with the holy thoughts and actions which his heart prompts and in which he delights]** (Proverbs 14:14, AMP).

Notice that the good man is satisfied from *himself* with his own holy thoughts and actions that are prompted by his heart.

You know, your husband or your wife is not the one who can make you happy and full of joy. Your spouse can certainly help make you happy. But when it comes right down to it, no one can affect what is on the inside of you except you.

If you want to walk with God and live in the joy of the Lord, you can do it. It doesn't matter what the circumstances are around you or how much pressure you face. You can be moved by God and His Word alone instead of what you see.

You may be facing trouble. Circumstances may not be getting any better. But what you do with the Word while you're walking through trouble determines the peace and joy you will experience despite the circumstances.

How do you walk joyfully in the midst of tribulation? You spend time in the Word. You meditate on the things of God. You depend on the Word for God's answers to your situation.

But what you *don't* do is look at the problem. When the problem becomes your focus, the joy of the Lord doesn't rise up in you and become your strength.

So as you go through your day, focus on the scriptures that give you the answer. Let all of your thoughts and your words center on what the Word says, not on what the circumstances look like.

Most people don't do that. Even when they pray, they focus on the problem. They tell God all about the problem in great detail, and that's the extent of their prayer.

There is a much more effective way to pray. Speak the Word in prayer. Tell God, "Father, I thank You for helping me. I'm not looking at the problem. I'm looking to You as my Source of deliverance. I'm looking at Your Word for my answer. The Word says so-and-so about my deliverance from this situation, and that's what I am standing on!"

When you focus on the Word, you can walk in the peace of God and the joy of the Lord through any test or trial. But focusing on the trial only causes you to walk in defeat. You won't have any supernatural help to bring you out of the trial because your faith is activated by the Word. When you are absorbed by the problem instead of the Word, you will always operate on a natural level.

You are responsible for keeping your own heart full of God's Word. The Scripture tells us to *set* our minds on things that are above (Colossians 3:2).

So if you want to get out of trouble and *stay* out of trouble, set your mind on heavenly things. Refuse to allow your problems to become your focus in life.

You may be facing a difficult situation in your marriage or in your finances. You may be experiencing problems with your children or your relatives. Whatever you are dealing with, go to God's Word and find scriptures to stand on in faith. Plant those divine promises in your heart. Speak them out of your mouth continually. Enter into thanksgiving for the answer that you believed you received when you prayed (Mark 11:23-24).

Keep your focus on what *God* said about your problem, not on the problem itself. When you're tempted to get discouraged or when a bad report comes your way, just hold fast to the Word of God. Set your affections — your focus, your attention — on the things above, and those adverse situations will pass away! A friend of mine said one of his favorite scriptures is **it shall come to pass!** (Deuteronomy 7:12).

You know, many times it looks as if there is no answer to a situation we face. I mean, it looks absolutely impossible — no way out, no solution.

But the truth is, you can't find a situation that God can't handle. As you hold fast to Him and release your faith in His Word, you will find out that God does have an answer for you.

The devil is the one who tells us there is no way out. But Jesus said, **I *am* the way** (John 14:6). All we have to do is keep our focus and stay vitally united to Him in faith until the answer is manifested.

Walking in Confidence Before God

Setting your mind on things above is what gives you supernatural peace in the midst of any storm of life. You can maintain that stance of faith with strength and confidence in honor to God and His Word. **In the reverent and worshipful fear of the Lord is strong confidence, and His children shall always have a place of refuge** (Proverbs 14:26, AMP).

Walking in the fear of the Lord gives you strong confidence that nothing else can give you. When you know your walk is pleasing to the Lord, something happens in your prayer life. When you talk to God, it's easy for you to expect Him to move.

But if you aren't living right, you *don't* have any confidence when you go before the throne of God. **Beloved, if our heart condemn us not, then have we confidence toward God. And whatsoever we ask, we receive of him,**

because we keep his commandments, and do those things that are pleasing in his sight (1 John 3:21,22).

When you walk before God in all the light you have, you can go boldly before the throne of grace with an assurance you can't obtain any other way. If you're walking in disobedience, you can't drum up that kind of confidence on your own. You may sound confident to others, but you won't be confident in your heart where it really matters.

Notice it says, **If *our heart* condemn us not** (1 John 3:21). It *doesn't* say, "If *God* condemns us not."

You see, if you are living contrary to God's Word, your family and your friends may not know it, but *you* will. And I guarantee you, when your heart condemns you, it weakens you greatly in prayer. It steals your confidence and causes your prayers to go unanswered.

But you can walk in the fear of the Lord with a clear conscience, giving Him honor in every area of your life. As you do, you will have *strong* confidence to boldly approach God's throne and receive help in time of need (Hebrews 4:16).

The Blessing of a Calm, Undisturbed Mind

There is a place in God where no storm disturbs the peace you have in Him. It is a place of supernatural peace because your mind and heart are fixed on Him: **A calm and undisturbed mind and heart are the life and health of the body, but envy, jealousy, and wrath are like rottenness of the bones** (Proverbs 14:30, AMP).

This verse is saying that the thoughts you think and how you conduct yourself with God affect the health of your body.

People who are always envious and jealous of others or who are full of wrath and anxiety are just inviting sickness and disease to take up residence in their bodies.

On the other hand, people who are calm and undisturbed are usually healthier. They have their hearts set on God, and they know that God is their Source and their Deliverer. When evil tidings come, they aren't moved by the bad report. They don't become agitated or live in anxiety and fear.

To abide in that place of rest — a place of continual, undisturbed peace and tranquillity — is something we should all be striving for in our spiritual walk. How do we attain such a place in God? By filling our heart with what our Father says about the situation so that out of our heart and mouth come only words of faith and deliverance. Every storm or trial looks small when we see things through God's eyes.

Wisdom for Today

*Determine to be moved by God and His Word alone
instead of what you see.*

*As you go through your day, focus on scriptures that give you the answer
to any problem you face.*

*Make sure you are walking before God in all the light you have so you can
approach His throne with strong confidence.*

CHAPTER 15
Instruction in Wisdom

You don't have to live in bondage to anger or any other sin of the flesh. By taking authority over sin and walking in God's wisdom, you set into motion a spiritual law that directs your path upward toward freedom and life.

❧

Proverbs Chapter 15

1 A soft answer turneth away wrath: but grievous words stir up anger.

2 The tongue of the wise useth knowledge aright: but the mouth of fools poureth out foolishness.

3 The eyes of the Lord are in every place, beholding the evil and the good.

4 A wholesome tongue is a tree of life: but perverseness therein is a breach in the spirit.

5 A fool despiseth his father's instruction: but he that regardeth reproof is prudent.

6 In the house of the righteous is much treasure: but in the revenues of the wicked is trouble.

7 The lips of the wise disperse knowledge: but the heart of the foolish doeth not so.

8 The sacrifice of the wicked is an abomination to the Lord: but the prayer of the upright is his delight.

9 The way of the wicked is an abomination unto the Lord: but he loveth him that followeth after righteousness.

10 Correction is grievous unto him that forsaketh the way: and he that hateth reproof shall die.

11 Hell and destruction are before the Lord: how much more then the hearts of the children of men?

12 A scorner loveth not one that reproveth him: neither will he go unto the wise.

13 A merry heart maketh a cheerful countenance: but by sorrow of the heart the spirit is broken.

14 The heart of him that hath understanding seeketh knowledge: but the mouth of fools feedeth on foolishness.

15 All the days of the afflicted are evil: but he that is of a merry heart hath a continual feast.

16 Better is little with the fear of the Lord than great treasure and trouble therewith.

17 Better is a dinner of herbs where love is, than a stalled ox and hatred therewith.

18 A wrathful man stirreth up strife: but he that is slow to anger appeaseth strife.

19 The way of the slothful man is as an hedge of thorns: but the way of the righteous is made plain.

20 A wise son maketh a glad father: but a foolish man despiseth his mother.

21 Folly is joy to him that is destitute of wisdom: but a man of understanding walketh uprightly.

22 Without counsel purposes are disappointed: but in the multitude of counsellors they are established.

23 A man hath joy by the answer of his mouth: and a word spoken in due season, how good is it!

24 The way of life is above to the wise, that he may depart from hell beneath.

25 The Lord will destroy the house of the proud: but he will establish the border of the widow.

26 The thoughts of the wicked are an abomination to the Lord: but the words of the pure are pleasant words.

27 He that is greedy of gain troubleth his own house; but he that hateth gifts shall live.

28 The heart of the righteous studieth to answer: but the mouth of the wicked poureth out evil things.

29 The Lord is far from the wicked: but he heareth the prayer of the righteous.

30 The light of the eyes rejoiceth the heart: and a good report maketh the bones fat.

31 The ear that heareth the reproof of life abideth among the wise.

32 He that refuseth instruction despiseth his own soul: but he that heareth reproof getteth understanding.

33 The fear of the Lord is the instruction of wisdom; and before honour is humility.

Hidden Treasures

The last verse of Proverbs 15 tells us that **the reverent and worshipful fear of the Lord brings instruction in Wisdom** (v. 33, AMP). I want to look at some very important instructions in wisdom found in this chapter regarding a universal problem — yielding to fleshly anger. We'll talk about overcoming anger and other sins of the flesh that can keep families in bondage to sin from one generation to the next.

Take Authority Over Anger in Your Life

God's wisdom tells us how to avoid anger: **A soft answer turns away wrath, but grievous words stir up anger** (v. 1, AMP). A person who is slow to anger also avoids strife: **A hot-tempered man stirs up strife, but he who is slow to anger appeases contention** (v. 18, AMP). Those two scriptures right there provide enough instruction to save you a world of hurt!

Verses 2 and 4 in *The Amplified Bible* show the fruit of an angry man: **The tongue of the wise utters knowledge rightly, but the mouth of the [self-confident] fool pours out folly.... A gentle tongue [with its healing** power] is a tree of life, but willful contrariness in it breaks down the spirit** (vv. 2, 4, AMP).

You see, with our words we can either be a blessing or a curse to people.

We have a responsibility to think about what we are about to say before we say it. We are to be in control of our own thoughts and words: **The mind of the [uncompromisingly] righteous studies how to answer, but the mouth of the wicked pours out evil things** (Proverbs 15:28, AMP). That's important because man's wrath never produces God's righteousness: **He who foams up quickly and flies into a passion deals foolishly** (Proverbs 14:17, AMP).

You know, just because you open your mouth doesn't mean something has to come out! There is something between your voice and your brain that can work for you — it's called your heart, your spirit man! You can learn to control yourself when you're tempted to "foam up quickly and fly into a passion." Your spirit can arrest those fleshly, angry words before your mouth pours out evil.

Many times in a family an uncontrollable temper is passed down from generation to generation. Dad has a bad temper, so his son has a bad temper too. Mother has a bad temper, so her daughter learns that same trait.

But you don't have to pass on your bad temper to your children. And you don't have to yield to it yourself, speaking out hurtful and foolish things you will later regret.

You can control your temper. Stop and speak to yourself when you're about to "pour out folly" in anger. Command your flesh to line up with God's Word in Jesus' name.

The devil will try to tell you, "Well, that's just the way you are. That anger is a part of your personality." But that isn't true. You've been re-created in Christ. You don't have to allow anger to attach itself to your life any longer.

Stop Generational Sins of the Flesh

God's power can put a stop to sins of the flesh that are prevalent in your family and have kept you in bondage in your own life.

You've been born again. Old things have passed away (2 Corinthians 5:17). Sin has lost its dominion over you (Romans 6:14). You don't have to carry on your family's sinful trait to your children. You can stop every evil tendency with the Word of God and the name of Jesus!

You have authority over the evil spirits that have followed your family for generations. It could be a spirit of alcohol or anger or gambling or stinginess. Whatever spirits have harassed your family, take authority over them in your own life. Otherwise, you will pass that sin right on to your children, and they will deal with the same problem as they grow into adulthood.

I once heard a minister say something interesting as he was teaching along this line. He made the comment that the same evil spirits that drove you to sin before you were born again will continue to try to control your life even after you're saved.

For example, if you were once an alcoholic, the same spirit of alcohol may try to tempt you in your spiritual walk. You may even walk closely with God for many years before that spirit suddenly tries to return to make you stumble.

You ought to know what kinds of evil spirits to watch out for in your life. You can probably look at the tendencies in yourself and your other family members and see what sins have been passed down from one generation to the next.

If sinful tendencies try to reestablish a foothold in your life again, refuse to give in to them. You don't have to pass those sins on to your children. You can stop those sins of the flesh right now in the name of Jesus by the power in His blood! That sin doesn't have any authority over you any longer. You don't have to let it back into your life.

The minister who was teaching about this subject said that in his family, the problem was lust. When he was growing up, his father would run off with a woman, come home for a few days and then leave to run off with another woman.

The minister said, "Through the years, I could see that my brothers and sisters were being pushed by that same spirit. Every member of our family eventually got divorced, and lust was the reason every one of those marriages broke up.

"So when I got married, I determined that the spirit of lust wasn't going to enter my household. I wasn't going to pass that sin on to my children. I took authority over that spirit, and my family has never had the problems the other family members have experienced."

That's what you must do in your life. Just determine, "I'm not going to let any sin have a hold on me. Sin is not going to be passed down my family line any further. I'm stopping it at my household. I may not be able to stop this sin in anyone else's household, but in the name of Jesus I can stop it in mine!"

Man, Not God, Sets Spiritual Laws Into Motion

It's crucial to your family's welfare that you make the decision to stop sin from taking up residence in your home. If you don't, spiritual laws can be set into motion that will result in heartache and trouble for your entire household.

Those spiritual laws also create a great contrast between the lives of the righteous who choose to forsake sin and the wicked who embrace it: **In the house of the [uncompromisingly] righteous is great [priceless] treasure, but with the income of the wicked is trouble and vexation** (Proverbs 15:6, AMP).

Now, it's important to understand that it isn't God Who punishes the sinner. He isn't causing this great contrast between the turmoil, vexation and fruitless end of the wicked and the many blessings enjoyed by the righteous.

God isn't watching people so that as soon as they do something wrong, He can punish them with some hurtful consequence. God doesn't do that. People set spiritual principles and laws into motion themselves by their own actions and choices (Proverbs 1:31).

The same principle holds true for the upright who obey God's Word. These people set spiritual laws into motion that cause good and blessing to come into their lives. They reap abundant life: **The path of the wise leads upward to life, that he may avoid [the gloom] in the depths of Sheol (Hades)** (Proverbs 15:24, AMP).

You see, when you walk in wisdom, *you* are the one who makes your way prosperous. You yourself set into motion the spiritual laws that determine your favorable outcome.

Isn't it a blessing to know that? Most people in this world don't know the Word of God. Most aren't aware of God's spiritual laws that produce either blessing or cursing in their lives.

But you *are* aware. You can make the right choice. You can walk in God's wisdom and avoid problems and trials.

Now, that doesn't mean you won't ever have any problems. But when you walk with God, problems won't have *you*. When problems come against you, you'll walk through them. You'll overcome them.

You have God's promise that the righteous will flourish and be blessed. He promises that the just shall come out of every trouble (Psalm 34:19).

Yes, we still go through some pressures and problems in this life. But we can know that as we walk with God, we will overcome, and our end will be victory! We have set into motion the right spiritual laws!

These are just a few of the many instructions in wisdom found in Proverbs 15. We receive those divine instructions by humility and the reverential fear of the Lord: **The reverent and worshipful fear of the Lord brings instruction in Wisdom, and humility comes before honor** (Proverbs 15:33, AMP).

When a person walks in his own conceit, he thinks he knows it all. That prideful attitude shuts him off from receiving God's wisdom.

On the other hand, when you walk in humility, your entire attitude is open to the Lord. You *want* Him to give you wisdom and correction.

So open your heart and humbly take instruction from the One Who is made unto you wisdom (1 Corinthians 1:24, 30). Resist anger and every other sin of the flesh that would try to hold you in bondage. Walk in the fear of the Lord, and set into motion the spiritual laws that cause priceless blessings of God to pour into your life!

Wisdom for Today

Stop and think about what you're going to say to someone before you say it.
Are you about to "utter knowledge rightly" or "pour out folly"?

Take authority over any evil spirits that have
followed your family for generations.

Be especially watchful for any temptation in areas of past weakness.
When one shows up, resist it in Jesus' name!

CHAPTER 16
Principles of Divine Direction

As you commit your ways wholly to the Lord and let peace rule in your heart, God causes your thoughts to become agreeable to His will. That's how your plans become established and succeed!

Proverbs Chapter 16

1 The preparations of the heart in man, and the answer of the tongue, is from the Lord.

2 All the ways of a man are clean in his own eyes; but the Lord weigheth the spirits.

3 Commit thy works unto the Lord, and thy thoughts shall be established.

4 The Lord hath made all things for himself: yea, even the wicked for the day of evil.

5 Every one that is proud in heart is an abomination to the Lord: though hand join in hand, he shall not be unpunished.

6 By mercy and truth iniquity is purged: and by the fear of the Lord men depart from evil.

7 When a man's ways please the Lord, he maketh even his enemies to be at peace with him.

8 Better is a little with righteousness than great revenues without right.

9 A man's heart deviseth his way: but the Lord directeth his steps.

10 A divine sentence is in the lips of the king: his mouth transgresseth not in judgment.

11 A just weight and balance are the Lord's: all the weights of the bag are his work.

12 It is an abomination to kings to commit wickedness: for the throne is established by righteousness.

13 Righteous lips are the delight of kings; and they love him that speaketh right.

14 The wrath of a king is as messengers of death: but a wise man will pacify it.

15 In the light of the king's countenance is life; and his favour is as a cloud of the latter rain.

16 How much better is it to get wisdom than gold! and to get understanding rather to be chosen than silver!

17 The highway of the upright is to depart from evil: he that keepeth his way preserveth his soul.

18 Pride goeth before destruction, and an haughty spirit before a fall.

19 Better it is to be of an humble spirit with the lowly, than to divide the spoil with the proud.

20 He that handleth a matter wisely shall find good: and whoso trusteth in the Lord, happy is he.

21 The wise in heart shall be called prudent: and the sweetness of the lips increaseth learning.

22 Understanding is a wellspring of life unto him that hath it: but the instruction of fools is folly.

23 The heart of the wise teacheth his mouth, and addeth learning to his lips.

24 Pleasant words are as an honeycomb, sweet to the soul, and health to the bones.

25 There is a way that seemeth right unto a man, but the end thereof are the ways of death.

26 He that laboureth laboureth for himself; for his mouth craveth it of him.

27 An ungodly man diggeth up evil: and in his lips there is as a burning fire.

28 A froward man soweth strife: and a whisperer separateth chief friends.

29 A violent man enticeth his neighbour, and leadeth him into the way that is not good.

30 He shutteth his eyes to devise froward things: moving his lips he bringeth evil to pass.

31 The hoary head is a crown of glory, if it be found in the way of righteousness.

32 He that is slow to anger is better than the mighty; and he that ruleth his spirit than he that taketh a city.

33 The lot is cast into the lap; but the whole disposing thereof is of the Lord.

Hidden Treasures

When I first started learning about God's Word, I didn't know what I know now about being led by the Holy Spirit. But one day I was studying Proverbs in *The Amplified Bible*, and I came across Proverbs 16:3. I knew I had found one of those priceless treasures of the Word!

In the years since then, the truth found in that scripture has helped me in my walk with God again and again. So we're going to "camp" on this verse for a while as we explore the principles of divine direction found in this chapter and throughout the Word of God.

Roll Your Works Upon the Lord

When I first discovered Proverbs 16:3, I was so excited to find such a wonderful key to receiving God's direction in my life! This is what it says in *The Amplified Bible*: **Roll your works upon the Lord [commit and trust them wholly to Him; He will cause your thoughts to become agreeable to His will, and] so shall your plans be established and succeed.**

At that time, I didn't have much confidence in my ability to make wise decisions. God was just beginning to teach me about listening to my heart. So I took this scripture and began to use it in my life and expect God to give me His thoughts. It worked for me!

Roll your works upon the Lord. Now, that's a crucial first step. The rest of the verse will never happen if you don't do that first. You have to *wholly* commit and trust them to Him. You have to maintain an attitude of trust in order to walk in this verse. First Peter 5:7 says, **Casting all your care upon him; for he careth for you.** You can't be worried. Roll the care all over on Him and expect your thoughts to become agreeable to His will. Then you can expect Him to cause your thoughts to become agreeable to His will, and your plans will become established and succeed!

Of course, this won't work if you aren't living for God. You can't live a godless life and still expect your thoughts to become agreeable to God's thoughts. But when you seek after God, walking in all the light you have and spending time in His Word, you can expect God to give you His thoughts. That's how He communicates with us in our walk with Him.

In other words, as we seek God and give Him place in our thoughts, He puts His thoughts on the inside of us. Then His thoughts rise from our spirit (heart) into our mind.

Many times, you may wonder whether the thoughts you are thinking are yours or His. But if you'll pay attention to your heart, something deep down inside of you will let you know His thoughts from yours. You'll just know.

For example, if you're about to embark in a direction that isn't agreeable to God's will, you'll sense a scratching, an uneasiness, a lack of peace down in your spirit. When you sense that uneasiness, stop and find out why it's there. The Holy Spirit is trying to tell you something. Take time and listen.

That's the way I walk through life. I won't make a major decision if I have uneasiness concerning God's will on the matter. Many times that makes me slower than others in getting something done, but it's worth it.

On the issues of life, I want peace in my heart. And if the matter is critical or involves something that could change the course of my life, I want more than peace. I want positive assurance to confirm the way He wants me to go.

But in most of my everyday life, I follow that sense of peace in my heart. I expect God to make my thoughts agreeable to His will. I expect Him to give me direction.

Let Peace Rule in Your Life

About the time I first discovered Proverbs 16:3, I found another scripture that goes along with it. Both of these verses together taught me how to follow the Lord's leading even before I really understood what I was doing.

The second scripture I found that helped me was Colossians 3:15 (AMP): **And let the peace (soul harmony which comes) from Christ rule (act as umpire continually) in your hearts [deciding and settling with finality all questions that arise in your minds].**

God's peace is to continually act as an umpire in your heart and mind! Suppose you are considering taking a certain direction and you don't have peace about it. You just aren't sure what God's will is on the matter.

Well, if you don't have peace about the step you're about to take, *don't do it*. Spend time praying about it. (This is when praying in the spirit really helps. When you don't know, you need to be able to let the Holy Spirit give you utterance.) Hold it before the Lord until you know the right thing to do. Follow peace.

Now, that sense of peace isn't a strong, tangible feeling. It's something you have to watch and listen for.

Sometimes we describe the leading of the Holy Spirit in our hearts as an *unction* or an *inner witness*. We have to look inside our spirit and see what the Spirit of God is telling us to do.

That inner unction isn't a strong, powerful voice that knocks you out of bed in the morning and says, "You must do this or die!" Sometimes God does speak in an audible voice, but that method of divine communication seems relatively rare. In your everyday life, most of the time you will be led by the inward witness.

So before I knew much about the inward witness, I let the peace of God be the umpire in my heart. And even today, when I have peace about a decision, I have a tendency to go ahead and do it. But if I don't have peace about it, I'll hold off and wait until I know for sure what to do.

Sometimes I probably wait too long, but I have discovered over the years that God isn't in a hurry; therefore, I shouldn't be in a hurry either. (Best of all, I stay out of a lot of trouble by this method of making decisions!)

God Creates His Desires in You

Rolling your works on the Lord is a very important element of following Him. As you do that, He causes your thoughts to become agreeable to His will. This principle agrees with Proverbs 3:6, which says, **In all thy ways acknowledge him, and he shall direct thy paths.**

When you begin to order your life according to the Word of God, you'll find that most of what God has laid out for you to do are things that you desire to do. Actually, God creates the desire in you: **It is God Who is all the while effectually at work in you [energizing and creating in you the power and desire], both to will and to work for His good pleasure and satisfaction and delight** (Philippians 2:13, AMP).

So when you walk with God, your desires will normally flow *with*, not *against*, His desires. He will speak a thought into your heart, and it will be as if He turned His light on the situation. You'll think, *Wow! I never looked at it like that. Why didn't I think of that before? This is the answer!*

Well, that's God giving you His thoughts concerning that matter. Most of the time, God's thoughts that come up from your spirit to your mind are pleasant. You'll just know they are right. You'll say, "That sounds good to me. I see that."

Maintain a Grateful Heart

The last part of Colossians 3:15 (AMP) is also a very important key to flowing with God: **And be thankful (appreciative), [giving praise to God always].**

You know, it's hard to hear what God is saying in your spirit if you let little things irritate you all the time. When God's peace isn't ruling in your life, you're always stirred up about some outside circumstance. That's why it's so difficult to hear what is in your spirit.

But when you maintain a thankful, grateful heart, it's so much easier to hear what the Holy Spirit is saying down in your spirit. You get up in the morning, and you're grateful for the new day. You aren't mad at God because He didn't do more for you yesterday. You are grateful for what He *has* done.

God has already done so much for us. If He never did another thing, we'd still be grateful to Him for the rest of our lives. Yet He never stops blessing us.

That's why it's so important to maintain a grateful heart, focusing on all He does for us rather than on the little frustrations of life.

So if you have a tendency to let everything irritate you, it's time to overcome that tendency. I guarantee you, this world isn't perfect. And if you expect your days to flow perfectly with no bumps along the way, you'll always be frustrated and disappointed.

There will always be people in this world who try to stir you up to anger or don't treat you right. But you just need to walk right through all the irritations of life without letting them steal your peace.

I'm telling you, *fight to keep your peace*. That peace is so important to your well-being. Living in peace not only makes it easier to hear from God, but it keeps your body healthier.

Just let this be a challenge to you: Don't let the world or people or irritations steal your peace and joy. Don't let the devil fill your mind with unbelief, doubt, fear and worry. Learn to live from the inside out! Make it your goal that *nothing* will keep you from discerning the direction of God in your life. Let peace rule, no matter what is going on around you.

Stop Worrying

Worry is one of the biggest thieves of peace there is. It becomes a major problem when you fail to roll your works on the Lord.

I remember when I learned to quit worrying and to commit all my ways to the Lord. I had grown up in a family that didn't know it was possible *not* to worry. I mean, some members of my family were expert worriers!

Well, for several years after I was born again, I didn't have any teaching in the Word. But I had *The Amplified Bible*, so two of my friends and I would meet at least once a week to read our new *Amplified Bible* together.

We didn't have a teacher who could show us in the Word what we needed to know. And although we had received the Holy Spirit, we knew very little about the Bible ourselves.

My friends and I just began to read the Word together. Whenever we received a little light on a scripture, we'd act on it — and it would work for us! Actually, the principles we learned began to work in our lives before we ever comprehended how those principles fit into the whole plan of God.

Then I began to see that I couldn't have faith and worry at the same time, so I decided to quit worrying. For me, it was like an alcoholic coming off booze. I had to quit one minute at a time because worry was such a habit with me. Actually, I used to think if I didn't worry, I wasn't being responsible.

So every time a worried thought came to me, I would overcome it with the Word of God. I would push the thought away and quote from the Word. I just continued to do that minute by minute until eventually worry stopped being a habit with me. (That had to be the Holy Spirit prompting me to do that. I didn't know enough to figure it out on my own!)

Maybe worry isn't your problem. Perhaps your habit is strife. For instance, do you get all stirred up for the rest of the day when someone says something the least bit unkind to you?

Well, you can get rid of strife the same way I got rid of worry. If you have to, just start dealing with it a moment at a time. If you have to quote the Word fifteen times every thirty minutes to overcome strife, then do it.

Every time strife tries to attach itself to you, resist it and say, "I'm walking in the peace of God!" You'll be surprised at how much more pleasant your life will be.

You see, you'll always have the opportunity for worry and strife. You just have to make the decision to stay in peace no matter what. It's a vital step in learning to hear from God.

Walk in What You Already Know

We've already talked about the importance of walking in the fear of God. But I want to mention it here because it is also a vital principle in receiving direction from the Lord. Proverbs 16:6 (AMP) says, **By the reverent, worshipful fear of the Lord men depart from and avoid evil.**

You see, the reason you decide to overcome worry or strife or anything else that blocks your communication with God is that you have more reverence for God than you do for your own selfish desires. When you walk in the fear of God and you know the right thing to do, you will do what's right because you want to honor God.

Most believers are troubled *not* by the fact that they don't know the right thing to do, but because they aren't doing what they know to do.

Yes, there's a lot we *don't* know. But if we'd just do what we know to do, we'd be living on a much higher spiritual level today in our walk with God.

So do what you know to do to receive direction from the Lord. He wants to make your thoughts agreeable to His will, but that process just doesn't happen automatically. You must roll your works upon Him. You must rid yourself of anything that keeps you from hearing His voice. And you must walk in the fear of God, letting peace rule as umpire in your heart.

God has given you these principles of divine direction for a reason. He wants to help guide you not only through your daily life, but to your appointed destiny in Him!

Wisdom for Today

Commit every situation you are facing today to the Lord once and for all and refuse to take it back. Trust Him with your life.

Don't make a major decision until you are sure of God's will on the matter. Follow peace.

When a worried thought enters your mind, immediately replace it with a promise from God's Word.

CHAPTER 17
Stop Strife and Seek Love

In order to walk in God's wisdom and keep the door of your life closed to the devil, you must guard diligently against strife and seek diligently to love others.

Proverbs Chapter 17

1   Better is a dry morsel, and quietness therewith, than an house full of sacrifices with strife.

2   A wise servant shall have rule over a son that causeth shame, and shall have part of the inheritance among the brethren.

3   The refining pot is for silver, and the furnace for gold: but the Lord trieth the hearts.

4   A wicked doer giveth heed to false lips; and a liar giveth ear to a naughty tongue.

5   Whoso mocketh the poor reproacheth his Maker: and he that is glad at calamities shall not be unpunished.

6   Children's children are the crown of old men; and the glory of children are their fathers.

7   Excellent speech becometh not a fool: much less do lying lips a prince.

8   A gift is as a precious stone in the eyes of him that hath it: whithersoever it turneth, it prospereth.

9   He that covereth a transgression seeketh love; but he that repeateth a matter separateth very friends.

10   A reproof entereth more into a wise man than an hundred stripes into a fool.

11   An evil man seeketh only rebellion: therefore a cruel messenger shall be sent against him.

12   Let a bear robbed of her whelps meet a man, rather than a fool in his folly.

13   Whoso rewardeth evil for good, evil shall not depart from his house.

14   The beginning of strife is as when one letteth out water: therefore leave off contention, before it be meddled with.

15   He that justifieth the wicked, and he that condemneth the just, even they both are abomination to the Lord.

16   Wherefore is there a price in the hand of a fool to get wisdom, seeing he hath no heart to it?

17   A friend loveth at all times, and a brother is born for adversity.

18   A man void of understanding striketh hands, and becometh surety in the presence of his friend.

19   He loveth transgression that loveth strife: and he that exalteth his gate seeketh destruction.

20   He that hath a froward heart findeth no good: and he that hath a perverse tongue falleth into mischief.

21 He that begetteth a fool doeth it to his sorrow: and the father of a fool hath no joy.

22 A merry heart doeth good like a medicine: but a broken spirit drieth the bones.

23 A wicked man taketh a gift out of the bosom to pervert the ways of judgment.

24 Wisdom is before him that hath understanding; but the eyes of a fool are in the ends of the earth.

25 A foolish son is a grief to his father, and bitterness to her that bare him.

26 Also to punish the just is not good, nor to strike princes for equity.

27 He that hath knowledge spareth his words: and a man of understanding is of an excellent spirit.

28 Even a fool, when he holdeth his peace, is counted wise: and he that shutteth his lips is esteemed a man of understanding.

Hidden Treasures

The most hazardous weapon the devil uses against us is also the foremost enemy of love. I'm talking about *strife*. We're going to talk more about this in our discussion of Proverbs 17.

Seek Love —
Overlook the Offense

Strife means *vigorous or bitter conflict, discord and antagonism; to quarrel, struggle or clash; competition; rivalry*. This dangerous sin is an open door to the devil. It gives him license to bring confusion and evil into our lives.

The Bible tells us how to avoid strife: **He who covers and forgives an offense seeks love, but he who repeats or harps on a matter separates even close friends** (Proverbs 17:9, AMP).

So what is the answer to avoiding strife? Well, most importantly, you are to *yield to love*. If you want peace in your life, give peace to others. Walk in love. Be quick to forgive and overlook an offense. Don't repeat matters that cause strife.

We can also avoid strife through forgiveness: **Good sense makes a man restrain his anger, and it is his glory to overlook a transgression or an offense** (Proverbs 19:11, AMP).

You know, the devil will always try to make us think the way the world thinks. The world says, "If someone mistreats or insults you, the only 'macho' response is to give him one right between the eyes!"

That's because the devil operates and thrives on strife since strife gives him an open door. The Bible says that where there is strife, there is also confusion and every evil work (James 3:16). Satan likes that kind of atmosphere. It breeds evil.

The devil tries to cause us to think like the world thinks. He wants us to believe that we have to defend ourselves when we are insulted. He wants us to think, *I'm going to get the last word. I'll give that guy a piece of my mind!* But no one needs a piece of your mind and you should keep all you have!

The Bible says that it is to your glory to overlook an offense. It also says that you have good sense when you restrain your anger.

Actually, insults won't hurt you if you don't partake of them — if you refuse to allow them in your spirit. You can forgive the person and go on peacefully, knowing that you just exhibited wisdom. Not only did you respond in wisdom, but you are still free from the trap of the devil.

Stop Strife Before It Breaks Out

Let's look at another important key to getting rid of strife: **The beginning of strife is as when water first trickles [from a crack in a dam]; therefore stop contention before it becomes worse and quarreling breaks out** (Proverbs 17:14, AMP).

You will never have a happy home if you don't resist strife. You see, Satan wants to stop your faith from working, so he'll try to slip in the back way and trick you into opening the door of your life to him.

Getting you into strife gives him a way in. Strife may seem to start out small. But really there is no such thing as insignificant strife. Strife left unchecked will flood your life like a ugly torrent.

The enemy likes to bring you an opportunity to get into a conflict with someone, because he knows that the moment you step into strife, he can gain mastery over you. He uses strife to interrupt the flow of love in your life. And once he's gotten you out of love, then he can cancel out your faith because faith works by love (Galatians 5:6). Love is our commandment. Jesus said, **This is my commandment, That ye love one another, as I have loved you** (John 15:12).

So if you want to walk in the power and blessing of God, don't open the door to the devil through strife. You have to make up your mind, "I am putting strife out of my house and out of my life!"

This is the way you do it: At the very first hint of strife, *stop it*. Don't let someone else pull you into an argument. Instead, walk in love and forgiveness and **stop contention before it becomes worse.** (Proverbs 17:14, AMP).

It takes two people to get into strife, and you can decide *not* to get into it! You don't have to fit the description of the person in Proverbs 17:19 (AMP): **He who loves strife and is quarrelsome loves transgression and involves himself in guilt....**

So when you recognize a situation that sparks feelings of aggravation, jealousy or strife within you, just look at that situation through the eyes of God and talk to it. Say, "I refuse to allow this situation to bring strife into my life. I yield to the forces of love and joy within me."

Stop Strife in the Home

Proverbs 17:1 (AMP) gives you more insight into the danger of strife in your home: **Better is a dry morsel with quietness than a house full of feasting [on offered sacrifices] with strife.**

The home is one of Satan's biggest targets. He continually tries to disrupt families by causing strife and division in their homes.

Your family is a powerful force for God when you're all in agreement with one another. That's why it's so important to stay out of strife and walk in love at home.

Oddly enough, home is often the most difficult place to be loving! I think the reason for that is we don't have our guard up when we're at home. We're not worried about our reputation. We're not trying to impress anyone. At home, we relax and nothing stops us from being selfish except our commitment to walk in the love of God.

But don't be fooled into thinking that it doesn't matter how you act at home. It matters a great deal. In fact, years ago the Lord said this to me, "If you allow Satan to stop you with strife at your front door, you'll be no threat to him anywhere else."

Don't Spread Strife Among Brothers

Let me warn you that as soon as you start putting strife out of your home, the devil will pressure you even harder to get into strife somewhere else — at work, at church — just anywhere will work for him. He'll provoke someone to be rude to you or hurt your feelings. Or he'll make sure you find out about other believers' mistakes, then try to convince you to talk about their mistakes to others.

When the enemy presents you with that opportunity, turn him down — *fast!* Treat that temptation to gossip and stir up strife as you would a poisonous snake. Turn your back and run the other way, because in the eyes of God, participating in strife is one of the most serious of sins.

We already read Proverbs 6:16-19: **These six things doth the Lord hate: yea, seven are an abomination unto him: A proud look, a lying tongue, and hands that shed innocent blood, an heart that deviseth wicked imaginations, feet that be swift in running to mischief, a false witness that speaketh lies, and** *he that soweth discord among brethren.*

Think about that for a moment. God considers stirring up strife such a grave sin that He lists it alongside murder and lying!

So stay away from strife. Ask God to reveal to you if you've entered into strife even inadvertently. He may remind you of a time you passed along some gossip about someone else or criticized the pastor. If He does, repent and make a decision to be more conscious of avoiding that strife in the future.

A Quality Decision
To Stay Out of Strife

When Ken and I first received the revelation of the danger of strife, we realized that if we wanted to walk in the full measure of God's blessings, we would have to stay out of strife. We wouldn't be able to argue with people or fight back when people criticized us or wronged us. We'd have to respond in love.

So we made up our minds to put strife out of our family. We made up our minds to keep it out of our ministry. We absolutely refused to operate in strife. And we determined that if we did mess up and exchange harsh words, we would be quick to repent and keep the devil from gaining a foothold in our lives.

If you want to walk in God's wisdom and keep the door of your life closed to the devil, that's the kind of decision you'll have to make, too. So guard diligently against strife. Make the commitment to keep strife out of your life. See to it that your prayers prevail by staying in harmony with your family members as well as others.

The moment you slip up and get into strife, make it right. Go to the other person and say, "Please forgive me. I love you. I don't want to be in strife with you." Then tell the Lord, "Father, I repent of strife. I refuse to be a person of strife. I choose to walk in love."

You may have to repent quite a bit at first if you've developed habits that must be changed. But don't get disgusted with yourself and give up. Just keep acting on the Word. Stop strife — and yield to love!

The love of God has been shed abroad in your heart by the Holy Ghost. You are born of God to walk in His love.

Wisdom for Today

Be quick to forgive and overlook an offense.

At the very first hint of strife, stop it. Don't let yourself be pulled into an argument.

Make up your mind to put strife out of your family. Absolutely refuse to operate in strife.

CHAPTER 18
The Fruit of Your Mouth

If you don't like the way your life is going today, you can change your tomorrow by changing your words.

Proverbs Chapter 18

1 Through desire a man, having separated himself, seeketh and intermeddleth with all wisdom.

2 A fool hath no delight in understanding, but that his heart may discover itself.

3 When the wicked cometh, then cometh also contempt, and with ignominy reproach.

4 The words of a man's mouth are as deep waters, and the wellspring of wisdom as a flowing brook.

5 It is not good to accept the person of the wicked, to overthrow the righteous in judgment.

6 A fool's lips enter into contention, and his mouth calleth for strokes.

7 A fool's mouth is his destruction, and his lips are the snare of his soul.

8 The words of a talebearer are as wounds, and they go down into the innermost parts of the belly.

9 He also that is slothful in his work is brother to him that is a great waster.

10 The name of the Lord is a strong tower: the righteous runneth into it, and is safe.

11 The rich man's wealth is his strong city, and as an high wall in his own conceit.

12 Before destruction the heart of man is haughty, and before honour is humility.

13 He that answereth a matter before he heareth it, it is folly and shame unto him.

14 The spirit of a man will sustain his infirmity; but a wounded spirit who can bear?

15 The heart of the prudent getteth knowledge; and the ear of the wise seeketh knowledge.

16 A man's gift maketh room for him, and bringeth him before great men.

17 He that is first in his own cause seemeth just; but his neighbour cometh and searcheth him.

18 The lot causeth contentions to cease, and parteth between the mighty.

19 A brother offended is harder to be won than a strong city: and their contentions are like the bars of a castle.

20 A man's belly shall be satisfied with the fruit of his mouth; and with the increase of his lips shall he be filled.

21 Death and life are in the power of the tongue: and they that love it shall eat the fruit thereof.

22 Whoso findeth a wife findeth a good thing, and obtaineth favour of the Lord.

23 The poor useth entreaties; but the rich answereth roughly.

24 A man that hath friends must show himself friendly: and there is a friend that sticketh closer than a brother.

Hidden Treasures

꒰ ꒱

Few people realize the power they release just by speaking *words*. Proverbs 18 talks about the power of the tongue, both for good and for evil, and how we can unleash that power to effect good in our lives.

Filled With the Fruit of Your Mouth

꒰ ꒱

A man's [moral] self shall be filled with the fruit of his mouth; and with the consequence of his words he must be satisfied [whether good or evil] (Proverbs 18:20, AMP).

If you don't like the way your life is going right now, you are going to have to change. You see, God isn't going to change. The devil isn't going to change. And if the world changes, it's only going to be for the worse.

But *you* can change. You can begin to spend more time with God. As you draw closer to Him, in prayer and in His Word, your lips will begin to speak right words that will bring good things to pass in your life.

We know that our words have the ability to affect our future because the Scriptures say our tongue determines whether we reap death or life: **Death and life are in the power of the tongue, and they who indulge it shall eat the fruit of it [for death or life]** (v. 21, AMP).

You can cause either blessing or cursing to come into your own life through your tongue. With that one little member of your body, you can set into motion spiritual laws that will affect the course of your life either for good or for evil (James 3:1-12).

It's up to you to discipline your tongue and cause it to agree with God's Word. When you speak God's Word, you bring good into your life that neither the devil nor the world can stop.

Now you can understand why **He who guards his mouth and his tongue keeps himself from troubles** (Proverbs 21:23, AMP). Troubles can be the bitter fruit a person must eat (or the unpleasant consequences a person must experience) when he *doesn't* discipline his mouth to agree with God's Word. For example, the Bible says a fool is someone who speaks whatever is on his mind: **A [self-confident] fool's mouth is his ruin, and his lips are a snare to himself** (Proverbs 18:7, AMP).

What You Say Is Important

Obviously, words are very important to our success in life. We have already seen in Proverbs that there isn't much promise for a fool. But the Bible says even the fool has more hope than someone who is hasty with his words (Proverbs 29:20).

So if you love life, you will guard your tongue: **For he that will love life, and see good days, let him refrain his tongue from evil, and his lips that they speak no guile** (1 Peter 3:10).

Whether or not you believe that words are powerful doesn't change the facts. What you say with your mouth does sow seed, and one day you will reap the harvest of that seed. So if you aren't happy with the way your life is today, put the Word of God in your mouth — and you'll see His desired results come to pass in your life.

When we speak God's Word, we know that we are going to come out right in the end. Make your words agree with what God says and with what you want to come to pass. If you don't want poverty and lack, don't speak it into your life with your words.

Your faith is released through your words. At times, that can be hard to do. For example, when the pressure is on and the bank account is low, you may become discouraged. You may be tempted to start talking lack and defeat. But don't give in to that. Just remember that God is your Source and like the psalmist says, **I have been young, and now am old; yet have I not seen the righteous forsaken, nor his seed begging bread** (Psalm 37:25).

Give Your Angels
Words to Hearken To!

God gives His angels charge over you to protect you, keep you and minister to you. They have been charged to hearken to God's Word spoken in faith (Psalm 103:20).

However, you have to put God's promises of deliverance in your heart and in your mouth to give the angels the voice of the Word they need to protect and deliver you. You have to refuse to speak words that are contrary to what you believe.

Jesus taught that your future is stored up in your heart: **For out of the overflow of the heart the mouth speaks. The good man brings good things out of the good stored up in him, and the evil man brings evil things out of the evil stored up in him** (Matthew 12:34-35, NIV). In fact He said, what you believe in your heart and say with your mouth, you will have in your life (Mark 11:23).

I know it is difficult for some to believe that our words carry this kind of power and authority. But here are two more places in Proverbs where this wisdom is given: **The wicked is snared by the transgression of his lips: but the just shall come out of trouble. A man shall be satisfied with good by the fruit of his mouth.... A man shall eat good by the fruit of his mouth: but the soul of the transgressors shall eat violence. He that keepeth his mouth keepeth his life: but he that openeth wide his lips shall have destruction** (Proverbs 12:13-14; 13:2-3).

Make it a practice to speak only words of faith. When you are under pressure, it will be tough sometimes — but you can do it! With practice it becomes normal for you to speak faith words instead of unbelief. When you answer every doubt and fear with what God's Word says about your situation, your angels will hearken to the voice of His Word and minister for you if you are an heir of salvation (Hebrews 1:14).

Wisdom for Today

If you don't like the way your life is going right now, change your words.

Discipline your tongue to agree with God's Word.

*Don't give in to discouragement. Continue to speak God's Word —
regardless of what you may feel or see.*

CHAPTER 19
Don't Blame Others — Examine Yourself!

When you find yourself in trouble, don't blame God or other
people — examine your own heart and actions. As you
honor God by doing what He tells you to do, He will lead you
out of trouble and cause His plan for your life to succeed!

Proverbs Chapter 19

1 Better is the poor that walketh in his integrity, than he that is perverse in his lips, and is a fool.

2 Also, that the soul be without knowledge, it is not good; and he that hasteth with his feet sinneth.

3 The foolishness of man perverteth his way: and his heart fretteth against the Lord.

4 Wealth maketh many friends; but the poor is separated from his neighbour.

5 A false witness shall not be unpunished, and he that speaketh lies shall not escape.

6 Many will intreat the favour of the prince: and every man is a friend to him that giveth gifts.

7 All the brethren of the poor do hate him: how much more do his friends go far from him? he pursueth them with words, yet they are wanting to him.

8 He that getteth wisdom loveth his own soul: he that keepeth understanding shall find good.

9 A false witness shall not be unpunished, and he that speaketh lies shall perish.

10 Delight is not seemly for a fool; much less for a servant to have rule over princes.

11 The discretion of a man deferreth his anger; and it is his glory to pass over a transgression.

12 The king's wrath is as the roaring of a lion; but his favour is as dew upon the grass.

13 A foolish son is the calamity of his father: and the contentions of a wife are a continual dropping.

14 House and riches are the inheritance of fathers: and a prudent wife is from the Lord.

15 Slothfulness casteth into a deep sleep; and an idle soul shall suffer hunger.

16 He that keepeth the commandment keepeth his own soul; but he that despiseth his ways shall die.

17 He that hath pity upon the poor lendeth unto the Lord; and that which he hath given will he pay him again.

18 Chasten thy son while there is hope, and let not thy soul spare for his crying.

19 A man of great wrath shall suffer punishment: for if thou deliver him, yet thou must do it again.

20 Hear counsel, and receive instruction, that thou mayest be wise in thy latter end.

21 There are many devices in a man's heart; nevertheless the counsel of the Lord, that shall stand.

22 The desire of a man is his kindness: and a poor man is better than a liar.

23 The fear of the Lord tendeth to life: and he that hath it shall abide satisfied; he shall not be visited with evil.

24 A slothful man hideth his hand in his bosom, and will not so much as bring it to his mouth again.

25 Smite a scorner, and the simple will beware: and reprove one that hath understanding, and he will understand knowledge.

26 He that wasteth his father, and chaseth away his mother, is a son that causeth shame, and bringeth reproach.

27 Cease, my son, to hear the instruction that causeth to err from the words of knowledge.

28 An ungodly witness scorneth judgment: and the mouth of the wicked devoureth iniquity.

29 Judgments are prepared for scorners, and stripes for the back of fools.

Hidden Treasures

꧁ ꧂

We talked earlier about the importance of receiving correction and maintaining a teachable spirit. Well, Proverbs 19 has some more light to shed on this subject to help us avoid common pitfalls in our walk with God.

The Danger of Blameshifting

꧁ ꧂

Proverbs 19:3 is a very enlightening scripture: **The foolishness of man subverts his way [ruins his affairs]; then his heart is resentful and frets against the Lord** (AMP).

You know, the day after Adam fell, he probably said to God, "Lord, why did You let this happen to me?" But God didn't let that happen to Adam. God told Adam exactly what His will was and what would happen if Adam disobeyed. He said, "Don't eat of the tree of the knowledge of good and evil, for the day you eat, you shall surely die" (Genesis 2:17, author's paraphrase).

People have such a tendency to blame God for their own mistakes. For instance, some people live in sin for years. They wouldn't give God the time of day. But when tragedy comes upon their household, they cry, "Why did God do this to me?"

God didn't do that to them — their own choices and lifestyles did! Spiritual laws were set in motion by the sin and death they lived in every day and by the words continually spoken from their heart and mouth. Those laws brought forth calamity that finally could not be averted.

We as believers often make the same mistake. We do stupid, unenlightened things and then blame *God*. For example, sometimes people enter into binding agreements with others that they shouldn't, just because they didn't take time to pray and find out what God wanted them to do. Then they ask, "God, why did You let this happen to me?"

In Hosea 4:6, God says, **My people are destroyed for lack of knowledge.** It is the foolishness of *man*, not the actions of God, that perverts man's ways and ruins his affairs.

If you find yourself in trouble, you'd better look first at yourself. The Bible says to **examine and test and evaluate your own selves to see whether you are holding to your faith and showing the proper fruits of it. Test and prove yourselves [not Christ]** (2 Corinthians 13:5, AMP).

So don't blame God for your situation. And don't try to blame your wife, your husband, your mother, your father or your children either.

It's easy to say, "Well, you know, it's my husband's fault. It's my wife's fault. It's my daddy's fault. God did this to me." But I'm telling you, people who always try to blame their problems on someone else are never happy people. They never grow up spiritually.

The only way you are ever going to improve the person you are today is to be brutally honest and frank about your own failures and shortcomings that need to be changed. If you always put the blame on someone else for your mistakes, you will never grow up in the Lord. Remember that no one is responsible for your life except you.

So examine your own heart and actions. Find out where you missed it. Look to see what you've done that is out of line with the Word, leaving the door open to the devil.

When the Lord reveals something to you, repent of your mistakes and make a decision to change. God will cleanse and strengthen you to put those weaknesses behind you. You don't have to repeat the same pattern of failure over and over again.

When you are willing to **hear counsel, receive instruction, and accept correction, that you may be wise in the time to come** (Proverbs 19:20, AMP), you can go on to victory. Why? Because instead of blaming others, you have judged yourself. Now you're ready to move on with God! **For if we would judge ourselves, we should not be judged** (1 Corinthians 11:31).

Wisdom in Disciplining
Your Children

The Bible says that **he who gains Wisdom loves his own life; he who keeps understanding shall prosper and find good** (Proverbs 19:8, AMP). Every time you honor God in your life and do what He tells you to do, you are really doing yourself good. You are causing God's blessings to come to you. That's true when you examine yourself rather than blaming others for your troubles. That's also true in every other area of your life.

For example, let's look at the area of disciplining your children for a moment: **Discipline your son while there is hope, but do not [indulge your angry resentments by undue chastisements and] set yourself to his ruin** (v. 18, AMP).

You honor God when you discipline your children. But you shouldn't discipline in anger or when your emotions are out of control. The key to disciplining your children is to be just. Don't allow yourself to discipline them when you're carried away with your own emotions. Deal with your children fairly and justly in a calm manner. Let them know what you are going to do beforehand and why you are doing it.

Children need discipline **while there is hope**. But you must be fair, and you must be right. You must be just and motivated by love. The key to peace between parents and children is the love of God. Children need continual assurance that they are loved so they understand that discipline is for their good. Listen to the Spirit of God. He'll tell you how to manage that balance in love and correction.

Let me give you another nugget of wise counsel about your children. Don't let the devil run roughshod over them as they grow into adolescence. When you see the first warning signs of rebellion in them, confess the promises of God over them. Refuse to give the devil any room to operate. Be quick to bring correction to them in love.

Remember, your children won't understand the unseen forces that are coming against them unless they are taught. Keep them in a good, strong church all their lives — a church that will teach them how to live according to

the Word. The most powerful advantage for good in your children's lives is to see to it that they are raised in the nurture and admonition of the Lord. Don't wait until you have a rebellious teenager to look to God for His help. If that is where you are, don't be discouraged. God will give you wisdom if you won't waver [James 1:5-6]. It's never too late with Him!

Children should be raised from birth to walk with God. In our church at Eagle Mountain, they are taught how to walk by faith, pray for one another and resist the devil. They are taught God's wisdom from the nursery. The parents are taught in the same way so that what they learn at church is continually reinforced at home. Our children are growing up choosing God. They aren't being forced into it. It is their choice because that's what they have been exposed to. They won't have any "wild oats" to sow as they mature because they are able to see through Satan's temptations and they know how to operate in the plan of God.

If you teach your children at home and live and talk right before them, they will grow up obeying God and resisting the devil.

As you honor God by raising your children according to His wisdom, you will reap the blessing of godly, obedient children!

God's Plan Will Stand

I'll give you another advantage of honoring God in your life. Your obedience to His Word can help you avoid the "school of hard knocks"!

Proverbs 19:21 (AMP) says, **Many plans are in a man's mind, but it is the Lord's purpose for him that will stand.** You know, you can learn that a wall is hard by butting your head against it, or you can take the word of someone who knows more than you.

In the same way, if you will go to the Word of God and learn from God's wisdom, you won't have to "butt against the wall of hard experience" to learn the lessons of life. You won't have to wait till you are old to be wise. You can learn from God's Word and become wise in your youth!

It seems like many don't have enough sense to do that. But the success and well-being of our lives is absolutely, totally bound up in the things of God.

Just because you are young doesn't mean you have to wait to become wise. You should be serious about growing and maturing and fulfilling the call of God on your life.

However, you *won't* fulfill that call if you make the mistake of ignoring God's Word: **Cease, my son, to hear instruction only to ignore it and stray from the words of knowledge** (v. 27, AMP).

How do you avoid that mistake? Well, instead of hearing and then ignoring instruction, do what God tells you to do. Rather than blaming others for your own shortcomings, examine yourself and deal with any open doors to the enemy in your life. That's how you honor God and cause His plan for your life to succeed!

Wisdom for Today

Don't blame God or other people for your troubles. Be honest
before God and examine yourself.

Discipline your children fairly and justly in love while there is still hope.
Live a godly life before them and teach them God's way of doing
and being right as early as possible.

Don't "butt against the wall of hard experience" to learn your lessons.
Let God's Word make you wise!

Drawing From God's Wise Counsel

*The Counselor Himself, the Holy Spirit, lives in your
spirit to lead and guide you — but you have to take
the time to draw out the deep waters of His counsel.*

Proverbs Chapter 20

1   Wine is a mocker, strong drink is raging: and whosoever is deceived thereby is not wise.

2   The fear of a king is as the roaring of a lion: whoso provoketh him to anger sinneth against his own soul.

3   It is an honour for a man to cease from strife: but every fool will be meddling.

4   The sluggard will not plow by reason of the cold; therefore shall he beg in harvest, and have nothing.

5   Counsel in the heart of man is like deep water; but a man of understanding will draw it out.

6   Most men will proclaim every one his own goodness: but a faithful man who can find?

7   The just man walketh in his integrity: his children are blessed after him.

8   A king that sitteth in the throne of judgment scattereth away all evil with his eyes.

9   Who can say, I have made my heart clean, I am pure from my sin?

10   Divers weights, and divers measures, both of them are alike abomination to the Lord.

11   Even a child is known by his doings, whether his work be pure, and whether it be right.

12   The hearing ear, and the seeing eye, the Lord hath made even both of them.

13   Love not sleep, lest thou come to poverty; open thine eyes, and thou shalt be satisfied with bread.

14   It is naught, it is naught, saith the buyer: but when he is gone his way, then he boasteth.

15   There is gold, and a multitude of rubies: but the lips of knowledge are a precious jewel.

16   Take his garment that is surety for a stranger: and take a pledge of him for a strange woman.

17   Bread of deceit is sweet to a man; but afterwards his mouth shall be filled with gravel.

18   Every purpose is established by counsel: and with good advice make war.

19   He that goeth about as a talebearer revealeth secrets: therefore meddle not with him that flattereth with his lips.

20 Whoso curseth his father or his mother, his lamp shall be put out in obscure darkness.

21 An inheritance may be gotten hastily at the beginning; but the end thereof shall not be blessed.

22 Say not thou, I will recompense evil; but wait on the Lord, and he shall save thee.

23 Divers weights are an abomination unto the Lord; and a false balance is not good.

24 Man's goings are of the Lord; how can a man then understand his own way?

25 It is a snare to the man who devoureth that which is holy, and after vows to make inquiry.

26 A wise king scattereth the wicked, and bringeth the wheel over them.

27 The spirit of man is the candle of the Lord, searching all the inward parts of the belly.

28 Mercy and truth preserve the king: and his throne is upholden by mercy.

29 The glory of young men is their strength: and the beauty of old men is the gray head.

30 The blueness of a wound cleanseth away evil: so do stripes the inward parts of the belly.

Hidden Treasures

Nothing should be more precious to us than the counsel of the Lord. That counsel holds the treasures of wisdom, peace, joy and prosperity that we need to walk in the fullness of God's life and blessings. So let's look in Proverbs 20 at some keys to receiving the counsel of the Lord. We'll use those keys to unlock other principles of divine direction!

The Deep Waters of God's Counsel

Let's look at one of those keys: **Counsel in the heart of man is like water in a deep well, but a man of understanding draws it out** (Proverbs 20:5, AMP).

Divine counsel comes to you from your spirit. The Counselor Himself, the Holy Spirit, lives in your spirit, but you have to *draw out* the deep waters of His counsel. You do that by giving God your attention as you spend time in His Word and in prayer.

If you are too busy to fellowship with God in the Word and prayer, then all of the hubbub and clamor of daily life can make it extremely difficult to hear the Holy Spirit's counsel in your spirit. You have to take the time to draw that counsel out. You have to listen.

You just can't stay busy with all the distractions of the world and still draw out what God is telling you to do. You have to get quiet in your spirit and listen to Him. When you get quiet and listen, you'll come to a place where you'll just know in your heart you've received the counsel of the Lord. You will have a "knowing."

The Candle of the Lord

Now let's look at another key verse for further insight into drawing out the Holy Spirit's counsel for our lives: **The spirit of man [that factor in human personality which proceeds immediately from God] is the lamp of the Lord, searching all his innermost parts** (Proverbs 20:27, AMP).

The *King James Version* calls the spirit of man **the *candle* of the Lord.**

You see, your spirit is where God's light of revelation comes to you. Out in the natural world that is ruled by darkness, you are surrounded by the lower thoughts of this earthly life. However, God's higher ways and thoughts reside within the deep well of your spirit. He gives you His thoughts, but those thoughts must be drawn out so understanding and wisdom can rise from your spirit and overcome natural knowledge to influence your thoughts.

That's what the psalmist meant when he said, **You cause my lamp to be lighted and shine; the Lord my God illumines my darkness** (Psalm 18:28, AMP). When you face a situation where you have to make a decision but you don't know what to do, God will enlighten your darkness. We even say "it just dawned on me," because it's as though a light is turned on, the answer is there and suddenly you know what to do. In other words, His counsel guides you in the way of wisdom so you can come through that situation in victory! **The light of the righteous rejoiceth** (Proverbs 13:9).

Jesus said, "Those who follow Me do not walk in darkness" (John 8:12, author's paraphrase). As believers we don't ever have to walk in darkness, because the Holy Spirit lights our candle with His revelation and illumines our darkness with the wisdom of God, **once hidden [from the human understanding] and now revealed to us by God** (1 Corinthians 2:7, AMP).

God has put His Spirit on the inside of us to reveal to us all that He has already done for us through Jesus Christ and to give us direction in our personal lives.

It's a sad state of affairs when people get born again, yet never know all that Jesus has wrought for their complete deliverance and salvation. For instance, believers can live their entire lives without learning that Jesus bore their sicknesses and carried their diseases (Matthew 8:17). Many never find out that God's Word promises deliverance from poverty.

In fact, a person can get born again and still live in poverty, lack and sickness the rest of his life. The only thing that will deliver him from such a fate is God's wisdom and counsel. That's why a wise man of understanding will draw from the deep waters of divine counsel and begin to live a higher way of life than those people just living in the natural realm.

With God's counsel, we can walk with Him in victory when there is turmoil all around us. We can be like the children of Israel.

The Israelites had light shining in their homes when darkness lay on the land of Goshen so thick that no one moved for three days! (Exodus 10:21-23). In the same way, the light of God's counsel can shine out of our spirits into a dark and confused world — a world where many people have no idea where they're headed in life.

You see, we aren't limited to what is going on in the natural realm. We can draw out the counsel of God and walk in His higher ways. He knows everything! He knows the past. He knows the future. He knows men's hearts.

We have to let go of the low life to take hold of the high life. We can't hold on to the sin we used to indulge in and still enter into God's realm of light, glory and victory. The Scripture warns us about this: **Whoever curses his father or his mother, his lamp shall be put out in complete darkness** (Proverbs 20:20, AMP). Sin can snuff out the candle of our spirit, making it almost impossible to hear the Holy Spirit when He tries to lead and guide us.

Sin desensitizes us so that we don't hear God speak to us. Remember the overcrowded heart? Cares of this world, deceitfulness of riches, lusts of other things enter into the heart and choke the Word. *The Amplified Bible* says they "suffocate" the Word. The Word in the heart then becomes "fruitless" or nonproductive (Mark 4:19). The less cluttered your heart is, the more sensitive you are to God.

That's why we have to fling those weights and sins aside and take hold of God's counsel. In His higher life are liberty, healing, deliverance and abundance. Drawing from His wise counsel causes us to live continually in the blessings of God. When you live in the blessings, you don't need miracles! Everything is already provided.

God Orders Our Steps

We all need God's counsel to order our steps. That's the only way we're going to make it successfully through life! Proverbs 20:24 (AMP) confirms this: **Man's steps are ordered by the Lord. How then can a man understand his way?**

I learned something interesting about the word "man" in this verse. The first time it's used, the word "man" comes from the Hebrew word *geber*, which means *strong man*. The second time "man" is used, it is translated from the Hebrew word *adam*. That word means *ordinary man*.[1] So this scripture actually reads like this: "A *strong man's* steps are ordered by the Lord. How then can an *ordinary man* understand his way?"

We just can't understand life without God. There is nothing to dispel the darkness without His light. We need to draw upon God's strength and counsel from within so He can order our steps! **The steps of a good man are ordered by the Lord: and he delighteth in his way** (Psalm 37:23).

The Honor of Ceasing From Strife

We already talked at length about strife. But here's a great nugget of wisdom about the subject of strife we can draw out of the counsel of God's Word and plant deep in our spirit: **It is an honor for a man to cease from strife and keep aloof from it, but every fool will quarrel** (Proverbs 20:3, AMP).

If only every one of us in the Body of Christ followed this wise counsel, we'd be so much further along in reaching the world with the gospel.

God says that it is an *honor* to cease from strife. Abraham is an example of a man who lived this verse (Genesis 13:5-12). Abraham and Lot were having trouble because of the strife among their servants. The servants argued with each other about grazing rights for their masters' sheep.

---

[1]*The Companion Bible* (Grand Rapids: Kregel Publications, 1990), p. 892.

Abraham told Lot, "Let there not be any strife between us. Look out on the land, Lot, and pick wherever you want to go with your family, flocks and servants. I will take what you don't want."

Abraham said, "We aren't going to fight over the land. We are going to cease from strife."

Now, the world would say, "Well, Abraham just backed down because he was weak." No, according to God, it was an honor for Abraham to avoid strife with Lot. And God honored Abraham for choosing a way that avoided strife. Instead of coming out of the situation a weaker man, Abraham went on to become even more prosperous and blessed than he was before!

You'll end up blessed, too, if you avoid strife as Abraham did. Draw the wise counsel of the Lord from your heart as you would draw water from a well. Wisdom comes from your heart to your head.

Let Him order your steps through every situation of life. Then when you confront a potentially strife-filled situation, do the honorable thing: Cease from strife and walk in the counsel of the Lord!

Wisdom for Today

Take the time to draw out the Holy Spirit's counsel from inside of you.
Spend time in the Word and in prayer, and listen.

When you face a situation where you don't know what to do, confess,
"God lights my candle and enlightens my darkness!"

Make the decision to let go of the low life of the world so you can walk in
the light and take hold of the high life of God!

CHAPTER 21
God Looks at the Heart

Man looks at the outward appearance, but God looks on your heart. That's why He believes in you so much. He knows you can do what He's called you to do. You've got the heart for it!

Proverbs Chapter 21

1 The king's heart is in the hand of the Lord, as the rivers of water: he turneth it whithersoever he will.

2 Every way of a man is right in his own eyes: but the Lord pondereth the hearts.

3 To do justice and judgment is more acceptable to the Lord than sacrifice.

4 An high look, and a proud heart, and the plowing of the wicked, is sin.

5 The thoughts of the diligent tend only to plenteousness; but of every one that is hasty only to want.

6 The getting of treasures by a lying tongue is a vanity tossed to and fro of them that seek death.

7 The robbery of the wicked shall destroy them; because they refuse to do judgment.

8 The way of man is froward and strange: but as for the pure, his work is right.

9 It is better to dwell in a corner of the housetop, than with a brawling woman in a wide house.

10 The soul of the wicked desireth evil: his neighbour findeth no favour in his eyes.

11 When the scorner is punished, the simple is made wise: and when the wise is instructed, he receiveth knowledge.

12 The righteous man wisely considereth the house of the wicked: but God overthroweth the wicked for their wickedness.

13 Whoso stoppeth his ears at the cry of the poor, he also shall cry himself, but shall not be heard.

14 A gift in secret pacifieth anger: and a reward in the bosom strong wrath.

15 It is joy to the just to do judgment: but destruction shall be to the workers of iniquity.

16 The man that wandereth out of the way of understanding shall remain in the congregation of the dead.

17 He that loveth pleasure shall be a poor man: he that loveth wine and oil shall not be rich.

18 The wicked shall be a ransom for the righteous, and the transgressor for the upright.

19 It is better to dwell in the wilderness, than with a contentious and an angry woman.

20 There is treasure to be desired and oil in the dwelling of the wise; but a foolish man spendeth it up.

21 He that followeth after righteousness and mercy findeth life, righteousness, and honour.

22 A wise man scaleth the city of the mighty, and casteth down the strength of the confidence thereof.

23 Whoso keepeth his mouth and his tongue keepeth his soul from troubles.

24 Proud and haughty scorner is his name, who dealeth in proud wrath.

25 The desire of the slothful killeth him; for his hands refuse to labour.

26 He coveteth greedily all the day long: but the righteous giveth and spareth not.

27 The sacrifice of the wicked is abomination: how much more, when he bringeth it with a wicked mind?

28 A false witness shall perish: but the man that heareth speaketh constantly.

29 A wicked man hardeneth his face: but as for the upright, he directeth his way.

30 There is no wisdom nor understanding nor counsel against the Lord.

31 The horse is prepared against the day of battle: but safety is of the Lord.

Hidden Treasures

Since none of us is perfect at following God's ways, I for one am glad for scriptures like this one: **Every way of man is right in his own eyes, but** *the Lord weighs and tries the hearts* (Proverbs 21:2, AMP). You see, God doesn't sit up in heaven and grade us by our natural talent or our performance; He looks to see what is in our *hearts*. That's the principle we're going to focus on as we go through Proverbs 21.

God's Search for a Devoted Heart

The Bible says that God doesn't see as man sees (1 Samuel 16:7). Although man looks at the outward appearance, God looks on a person's heart. That's why many times God chooses a person to do a work that we would never choose. We'd look at the outward man and say, "What does that person have to offer?" But God looks at the heart.

To tell you the truth, you look a whole lot better in your heart than you do in your outward appearance! That's why God believes in you so much.

Sometimes you may think, *God, why do You even put up with me? What makes You think I could ever do what You're telling me to do?*

But when God calls you to do something, He doesn't look at what you are in the flesh. He doesn't make decisions according to your natural talent or ability. Those factors don't really mean much to God, because He already has all the talent and ability needed to get the job done. He knows that He can put His ability inside of you so you can fulfill what He has asked you to do.

God looks at your heart, because the condition of your heart determines what He can or cannot do with your life. You live and move and have your life from your *heart*, not from your natural limitations. You (the real you) are a spirit. You live in a body. You have a soul (your mind, will and emotions).

That's why God expects so much from you. He knows you can do what He's called you to do when your heart (spirit or inner man) belongs to Him. Your real potential is in your heart. That's where God dwells (2 Corinthians 6:16).

The 'Perfect' Heart

God is looking for people to do His work on the earth with willing, devoted hearts. In fact, the Bible says that **the eyes of the Lord run to and fro throughout the whole earth, to show himself strong in the behalf of them whose heart is perfect toward him** (2 Chronicles 16:9).

That word "perfect" doesn't imply that God is looking for those who never make a mistake. The Hebrew meaning of "perfect heart" is a heart that is devoted, consecrated, loyal and faithful to Him.

That's the reason God is always there to help us get back up after we stumble and fall. We may make mistakes or wrong decisions; we may follow the flesh and do something wrong. But if our hearts desire to do what's right before God, then no matter how many mistakes we make, God will always help get us back on track. (Of course, if we keep making mistakes on purpose, then our hearts aren't right before God!)

So we shouldn't get discouraged when we recognize that we made a mistake and somehow got out of the will of God. We just need to repent and go on from there. God doesn't keep track of our mistakes; He looks at the thoughts and intents of our heart. He works with hearts.

A Proud Heart

With that truth in mind, let's look now at some other verses in Proverbs 21 that show the different types of hearts people can have. The first one is a proud heart. The Scripture tells us that **haughtiness of eyes and a proud heart** are sin in the eyes of the Lord (v. 4, AMP).

I don't know anything that will stop wisdom more quickly from operating in your life than a proud, haughty heart. In fact, one of the secrets of staying in the will of God and keeping yourself on track is that you *don't overestimate yourself*. Remember, **pride goeth before destruction, and an haughty spirit before a fall** (Proverbs 16:18). That is truly a word of wisdom.

Just remind yourself once in a while of the many times in the past you have floundered around making every mistake imaginable, but God's tender mercies pulled you through. Don't let those thoughts condemn you; just let them keep you dependent and humble. God hates a proud heart — the spirit that overestimates oneself and underestimates others (Proverbs 6:17).

The Patient Heart

One thing God really works with is a *patient* heart. Patience is absolutely required to grow in the things of God.

The danger of impatience is that **everyone who is impatient and hasty hastens only to want** (Proverbs 21:5, AMP). Why is that? Because faith will fail without patience.

James 1:4 tells us that in the midst of tests and trials, we are to **let patience have her perfect work, that ye may be perfect and entire, wanting nothing.**

When you are tempted to cave in and faint, let patience have her perfect work. As you patiently hold fast to your faith in the midst of every trial you face, you will be on your way to becoming mature, full-grown, entire and lacking in nothing. What a place!

The Wise Heart
Versus a Scoffer's Heart

Now let's look at a verse that shows two different kinds of hearts — the scoffer's heart and the wise man's heart: **When the scoffer is punished, the fool gets a lesson in being wise; but men of [godly] Wisdom and good sense learn by being instructed** (Proverbs 21:11, AMP).

A scoffer is one who mocks or derides the things of God. He despises what is good. And when a scoffer is punished because of his own rebellious heart, the fool gets a lesson in how to be wise. Now, after all we've heard about fools in the book of Proverbs, that's saying a mouthful!

On the other hand, men of wisdom (that's supposed to be us!) learn by being instructed. In other words, we aren't supposed to learn by hard experience. The best teacher is God's Word as revealed to us by the Spirit of God.

As a person of wisdom, you can sit under teachers of the Word who have already walked the path you're walking and have learned truths about God along the way. You can even learn from the mistakes they made. You'll be able to start at a place in your spiritual walk that took them years to attain because they had so much to learn on their own.

You can be one of the wise of heart. You don't have to learn by making a lot of mistakes yourself. You don't have to be beaten up and pushed down by circumstances because you did things your own way.

Instead, you can receive wisdom from God and walk in obedience to His Word. You can avoid a host of problems and trials you would otherwise have gone through.

So make the decision to be a person of wisdom and good sense. Keep your heart open to the instruction of the Word. Make a decision: "God is smarter than I am. I'm going to do whatever He says."

Nothing Can Prevail
Against God's Wisdom!

The wisdom that comes from above comes directly from the Lord into your heart. Among other things, that heavenly wisdom is **first pure, then peaceable, gentle, and easy to be entreated, full of mercy and good fruits, without partiality, and without hypocrisy** (James 3:17).

On the other hand, the wisdom of the world is earthly, devilish and sensual (James 3:15). However, the Bible says **there is no [human] wisdom or understanding or counsel [that can prevail] against the Lord** (Proverbs 21:30, AMP).

So when we stand on God's Word, the devil can't prevail against us. Our enemies can't prevail against us. God tells us, **they who war against you shall be as**

nothing, as nothing at all. For I the Lord your God hold your right hand; I am the Lord, Who says to you, Fear not; I will help you! (Isaiah 41:12-13, AMP).

There isn't any counsel, enemy, opposition or threat that can prevail against you if you walk in the light and stand on the Word of God. It may look dark, and it may seem impossible. It may look like the world has every advantage over you. But darkness never overtakes light. You turn on the light and darkness flees.

When you walk according to the Word and your heart is right, then it doesn't matter what comes against you. *Nothing* can prevail against the wisdom of God. That is God's promise, and that is the security you have when you walk before Him with a pure heart!

Wisdom for Today

When you recognize that you made a mistake, just repent and go on. Remember, God isn't keeping track — He's looking at your heart.

Make sure you keep your heart devoted, consecrated, loyal and faithful to God, so that He can show Himself strong on your behalf.

When you are tempted to cave in and faint in the midst of a trial, hold fast to your faith. Let patience have her perfect work until you are entire lacking in nothing.

CHAPTER 22
The Rewards of Humility

When you walk in humility, you apply God's principles
of wisdom to your life because it brings honor to Him.
Such humility before God brings divine rewards —
but the greatest reward is found in pleasing Him!

Proverbs Chapter 22

1   A good name is rather to be chosen than great riches, and loving favour rather than silver and gold.

2   The rich and poor meet together: the Lord is the maker of them all.

3   A prudent man foreseeth the evil, and hideth himself: but the simple pass on, and are punished.

4   By humility and the fear of the Lord are riches, and honour, and life.

5   Thorns and snares are in the way of the froward: he that doth keep his soul shall be far from them.

6   Train up a child in the way he should go: and when he is old, he will not depart from it.

7   The rich ruleth over the poor, and the borrower is servant to the lender.

8   He that soweth iniquity shall reap vanity: and the rod of his anger shall fail.

9   He that hath a bountiful eye shall be blessed; for he giveth of his bread to the poor.

10   Cast out the scorner, and contention shall go out; yea, strife and reproach shall cease.

11   He that loveth pureness of heart, for the grace of his lips the king shall be his friend.

12   The eyes of the Lord preserve knowledge, and he overthroweth the words of the transgressor.

13   The slothful man saith, There is a lion without, I shall be slain in the streets.

14   The mouth of strange women is a deep pit: he that is abhorred of the Lord shall fall therein.

15   Foolishness is bound in the heart of a child; but the rod of correction shall drive it far from him.

16   He that oppresseth the poor to increase his riches, and he that giveth to the rich, shall surely come to want.

17   Bow down thine ear, and hear the words of the wise, and apply thine heart unto my knowledge.

18   For it is a pleasant thing if thou keep them within thee; they shall withal be fitted in thy lips.

19   That thy trust may be in the Lord, I have made known to thee this day, even to thee.

20 Have not I written to thee excellent things in counsels and knowledge,

21 That I might make thee know the certainty of the words of truth; that thou mightest answer the words of truth to them that send unto thee?

22 Rob not the poor, because he is poor: neither oppress the afflicted in the gate:

23 For the Lord will plead their cause, and spoil the soul of those that spoiled them.

24 Make no friendship with an angry man; and with a furious man thou shalt not go:

25 Lest thou learn his ways, and get a snare to thy soul.

26 Be not thou one of them that strike hands, or of them that are sureties for debts.

27 If thou hast nothing to pay, why should he take away thy bed from under thee?

28 Remove not the ancient landmark, which thy fathers have set.

29 Seest thou a man diligent in his business? he shall stand before kings; he shall not stand before mean men.

Hidden Treasures

We began this study on Proverbs by discussing the fear of the Lord. When you walk in the fear and reverence of God, you humble yourself to do what *He* says rather than what *you* might prefer to do. You are obeying what He says because it brings honor to Him. That is walking in humility, and that's what we're going to talk about in Proverbs 22.

Humility Toward God

God promises rewards for the humble in this life: **The reward of humility and the reverent and worshipful fear of the Lord is riches and honor and life** (Proverbs 22:4, AMP). Humility begins between you and God. Humility is first walking in submission and obedience to Him.

When you are humble toward God, you walk in the **reverent and worshipful fear of the Lord**. You are quick to do what He says. You are quick to let Him be God. You bow your knee before His will and what *He* desires in your life. You defer to Him.

Walking in humility includes obeying God's admonition to trust Him: **Lean on, trust in, and be confident in the Lord with all your heart and mind and do not rely on your own insight or understanding** (Proverbs 3:5, AMP).

You can see the quality of humility in that verse. When you're not leaning on your own understanding, you cease to be **wise in your own eyes** (Proverbs 3:7, AMP). And because you are walking in humility before God, you receive His grace and undeserved favor: **Though He scoffs at the scoffers and scorns the scorners, yet He gives His undeserved favor to the low [in rank], the humble, and the afflicted** (Proverbs 3:34, AMP). Pride shuts the door of God's favor. Humility opens wide the door of His favor.

We can find that same principle in 1 Peter 5:5. God sets Himself against the proud, but He gives grace (favor) to the humble.

Humility before God does bring financial rewards. But God's reward of material possessions is not our first priority.

God won't make you rich unless your priorities are in order. God's plan for us is abundance without covetousness, so we don't put our trust in material possessions, but in God Himself. Then if something happens to our material possessions, we're still intact because we didn't put our trust in the wrong thing. We know that the God Who blessed us the first time will bless us the second time as well, because *He* is our Source and our Supply.

So humbly seek God and His righteousness first, and He will add all His other blessings to you (Matthew 6:33). Really, the only safe way to be prosperous is to give the Lord first place in your life.

The enemy tries to use wealth and riches as a snare and a temptation: **They that will be rich fall into temptation and a snare, and into many foolish and hurtful lusts** (1 Timothy 6:9). But material wealth won't be a snare to those who seek first after God.

So walk in humility before God — not just so you can receive His reward of riches, honor and life, but because you love and honor Him as God. Don't seek to be rich — seek to be *holy*. When the motive of your heart is pure, God will add all the other blessings He has promised to your life.

The Word That Is Alive in You

Walking in humility means you listen and submit to God's words to the wise, applying your mind to His knowledge (Proverbs 22:17, AMP). As you submit and apply yourself to God's principles, He promises that **it will be pleasant if you keep them in your mind [believing them]; your lips will be accustomed to [confessing] them** (v. 18, AMP).

We are to keep God's principles of wisdom in our minds and hearts and make our lips accustomed to confessing them. As we do, God's wisdom will become pleasant to us and alive in us. In other words, we will continually enjoy the wisdom of God.

This verse is talking about making sure God's Word *abides* in us. Jesus told us that if we abide in Him and His words abide in us, we can ask what we will and it will be done for us (John 15:7).

You see, the Word that abides in you is the Word that is alive in you. When tests or trials come against you, that Word will be on deposit on the inside of you. It will rise up to help you when you need it.

You don't have to work at believing that the Word abides in you. The Word abiding within is pleasant knowledge because it's alive in your heart, and it causes your trust, belief, reliance, support and confidence to be in the Lord (v. 19, AMP).

God tells us to **forget not all his benefits** (Psalm 103:2). You see, it's the Word you remember that does you good. The benefits you forget aren't going to help you because you will not exercise faith in that area.

That's the reason we stay in God's Word. We don't just read it for a while when we are first born again. We continually keep hearing the Word so its truth abides in the midst of our hearts and stays current in our lives. The Word that is abiding in you is the Word that talks to you (John 15:7).

Training Up Your Children
According to the Word

꽃

All these principles of wisdom we're talking about are not only for your own good but for the good of your children. They will equip you to better **train up a child in the way he should go** (Proverbs 22:6).

I received some good insight about this verse in *The Companion Bible*. The word "train" in this verse means *to hedge in*, the way cowboys do when guiding cattle to a desired destination.[1]

That's our job with our children. We are to hedge them in by setting godly boundaries for their lives.

---

[1]*The Companion Bible* (Grand Rapids: Kregel Publications, 1990), p.894.

You are to train your children with the Word of God, teaching them first of all through the godly life you live before them. The truth is, if you live a holy life, you are the best letter from God they will ever read.

Your children won't ever forget the things they learn from you. Now, they may forget the words you say to them, but they won't forget the way of life you established in your home. They won't forget the times you prayed for them and they were healed. They won't forget that in times of trouble, the family turned to God, and God delivered them.

The Companion Bible definition gave me a broader understanding of the word "train" than I had understood before. As we "hedge in" our children with godly boundaries, we are to tell them, "Now, this is too far. You can't go over there. You have to stay within this scope of godly behavior." We are to guide our children to walk through life according to God's Word.

So it's up to us to obey the principles of wisdom God has set forth in His Word. As we do, we can expect the rewards of humility and obedience He has promised.

But don't seek after the reward — seek first after the Giver of the reward. I can tell you this for sure — knowing that you have pleased Him is the greatest reward of all!

Wisdom for Today

Be quick to do what God tells you to do. Bow your knee before
His will and what He desires for your life.

Keep God's principles of wisdom alive and fresh in your mind and heart.
Make it a habit for your lips to confess them.

Train your children with the Word of God, teaching them first of all through
the godly life you live before them, while you set boundaries for their lives
according to God's Word.

CHAPTER 23
God's Ways, Not the World's Ways

*We live in a very critical hour. Time is much too short
to waste playing around with sin. It's time to turn away
from evil and walk in the wisdom and ways of God.*

⁂

Proverbs Chapter 23

1   When thou sittest to eat with a ruler, consider diligently what is before thee:

2   And put a knife to thy throat, if thou be a man given to appetite.

3   Be not desirous of his dainties: for they are deceitful meat.

4   Labour not to be rich: cease from thine own wisdom.

5   Wilt thou set thine eyes upon that which is not? for riches certainly make themselves wings; they fly away as an eagle toward heaven.

6   Eat thou not the bread of him that hath an evil eye, neither desire thou his dainty meats:

7   For as he thinketh in his heart, so is he: Eat and drink, saith he to thee; but his heart is not with thee.

8   The morsel which thou hast eaten shalt thou vomit up, and lose thy sweet words.

9   Speak not in the ears of a fool: for he will despise the wisdom of thy words.

10   Remove not the old landmark; and enter not into the fields of the fatherless:

11   For their redeemer is mighty; he shall plead their cause with thee.

12   Apply thine heart unto instruction, and thine ears to the words of knowledge.

13   Withhold not correction from the child: for if thou beatest him with the rod, he shall not die.

14   Thou shalt beat him with the rod, and shalt deliver his soul from hell.

15   My son, if thine heart be wise, my heart shall rejoice, even mine.

16   Yea, my reins shall rejoice, when thy lips speak right things.

17   Let not thine heart envy sinners: but be thou in the fear of the Lord all the day long.

18   For surely there is an end; and thine expectation shall not be cut off.

19   Hear thou, my son, and be wise, and guide thine heart in the way.

20   Be not among winebibbers; among riotous eaters of flesh:

21   For the drunkard and the glutton shall come to poverty: and drowsiness shall clothe a man with rags.

22   Hearken unto thy father that begat thee, and despise not thy mother when she is old.

23   Buy the truth, and sell it not; also wisdom, and instruction, and understanding.

24 The father of the righteous shall greatly rejoice: and he that begetteth a wise child shall have joy of him.

25 Thy father and thy mother shall be glad, and she that bare thee shall rejoice.

26 My son, give me thine heart, and let thine eyes observe my ways.

27 For a whore is a deep ditch; and a strange woman is a narrow pit.

28 She also lieth in wait as for a prey, and increaseth the transgressors among men.

29 Who hath woe? who hath sorrow? who hath contentions? who hath babbling? who hath wounds without cause? who hath redness of eyes?

30 They that tarry long at the wine; they that go to seek mixed wine.

31 Look not thou upon the wine when it is red, when it giveth his colour in the cup, when it moveth itself aright.

32 At the last it biteth like a serpent, and stingeth like an adder.

33 Thine eyes shall behold strange women, and thine heart shall utter perverse things.

34 Yea, thou shalt be as he that lieth down in the midst of the sea, or as he that lieth upon the top of a mast.

35 They have stricken me, shalt thou say, and I was not sick; they have beaten me, and I felt it not: when shall I awake? I will seek it yet again.

Hidden Treasures

We live in a very critical hour. It is crucial that we walk in God's wisdom so things can go well in our lives. As this age draws to a close, time has been compressed. Evil has become more volatile around us. Time is much too short to waste playing around with sin.

Therefore, God's admonition not to associate with the ungodly is an extremely important message to heed. In Proverbs 23, that message comes through loud and clear. God wants us to follow His ways of wisdom, not the ways of the world.

The Dangers of Alcohol

Let's talk about one particular "way of the world": drinking strong drink. The Bible tells us about the dangers of alcohol: **Who has woe? Who has sorrow? Who has strife? Who has complaining? Who has wounds without cause? Who has redness and dimness of eyes? Those who tarry long at the wine.** (Proverbs 23:29-30, AMP).

The world tries to convince us, "Drinking alcohol is no big deal. Everyone is doing it." It's the same message the world uses to pull people into adultery and every other fleshly sin. But don't be deceived — drunkenness is an enemy.

Common and Acceptable?

In my generation, teenagers only drank on special occasions, such as graduation or prom night. But young people today have been raised in a generation in which drinking is the common, accepted thing to do.

However, no matter how common and accepted it is to drink alcohol, the practice is still just as deadly now as it was when the book of Proverbs was written. Alcohol will still ruin your life. It will still hold you in bondage with invisible chains that won't let you go. Just ask anyone who has tried without God's help to get free of the grip of alcohol.

That's why God says, **Do not associate with winebibbers** [or *drunkards*] (v. 20, AMP). The definition of "drunkard" is *a person who is often drunk.*

We often think of a drunkard as the man living on the street who carries a bottle in his hand and needs a shave and bath. But there are a lot of "acceptable" people by society's standards who fit the definition of a drunkard, yet would definitely *not* want to be labeled that.

Drinking Alcohol Is Not All Right

Now, you'd think that anyone who has walked with the Lord awhile would know that drinking alcohol isn't the right thing to do and that there is no future in it. But some pastor friends of mine once passed out a questionnaire to their large congregation. One of the questions they asked was, "Do you believe it is all right to drink alcohol?" More than 50 percent of this supposedly turned-on, fired-up, spirit-filled church responded, "Yes, we believe it's all right!"

You see, when Christians choose the society of the ungodly and the unbelieving, they expose themselves to temptation and become familiar with sin. And a believer's familiarity with sin will inevitably cause that sin to appear less repulsive to him. **Do not be so deceived and misled! Evil companionships (communion, associations) corrupt *and* deprave good manners *and* morals *and* character** (1 Corinthians 15:33, AMP).

But alcohol isn't all right! It will never do you good. And there is a chance it could totally ruin your life.

I was raised in a home where alcohol was prevalent, and I know what I'm talking about. Alcohol is a thief of the life of God. It is a thief of peace in the home. It is especially hard on children.

Drinking Strong Drink Isn't Wise

The Bible tells it like it is: **Wine is a mocker, strong drink a riotous brawler; and whoever errs or reels because of it is not wise** (Proverbs 20:1, AMP). You cannot be wise and be influenced by alcohol. You just have to come to grips with that fact. If you choose to go the way of alcohol, you have to let wisdom go, because drinking strong drink isn't wise.

I'll tell you one reason it isn't wise. You're in a spiritual war. There is an enemy prowling about trying to kill, steal and destroy everything good in your life. One of the worst things you can do when at war is to do something that will weaken your will or hinder your ability to fight. That's exactly what drinking alcohol does, both to a natural soldier and to a believer who has to deal with demonic forces that come against him.

The following scripture describes a person under the influence of strong drink: **Your eyes will behold strange things [and loose women] and your mind will utter things turned the wrong way [untrue, incorrect, and petulant]** (Proverbs 23:33, AMP).

In other words, you talk wrong, you think wrong and you act wrong when you are under the influence of alcohol. You just aren't in control of yourself the way you should be.

This should give you a clue as to its origin and how the devil uses this tool. With the devil it's all about control anyway. He lost his control and authority when Jesus paid the price for man's sin. Now Satan has to work through man to get anything done. Refuse to make yourself available.

Now, you may not see anything wrong with indulging in a little glass of wine after dinner now and then. But you have to admit that many others do think it's wrong, and we're under obligation to live right before other people. You may think no one will find out, but they will. Things can't stay a secret. Jesus said what is done in the dark is going to be made known in the light (Luke 12:3).

Maybe *you* can have just one glass of wine and never overindulge, but what about the people to whom you are an example? Wine is alcohol. It is addictive. It is easy for people to become alcoholics. You don't want to be responsible for that. The Bible says to avoid the very appearance of evil (1 Thessalonians 5:22).

You may say, "Well, I can drink alcohol and still go to heaven." But you can't do it and be wise. You can't do it and be successful in your walk with the Lord. And you can't do it and stay out of trouble.

You and I are disciples of the Lord Jesus Christ — not just pupils, but adherents to His commands. We are supposed to walk a straight walk according to God's Word and be an example of how to live godly in this present world.

Take Authority
Over the Enemy's Strategy

You may come from a family where alcohol has been a problem. Remember, many times spirits are handed down from generation to generation. So be aware that those same alcoholic spirits that harassed your father or your grandfather will probably try to go after you. It's up to you to take authority over those spirits in Jesus' name and cast them out of your family forever.

Just because alcohol has been a problem in your family doesn't mean it has to be a threat to you. But it does mean that if you are tempted or pulled in that direction, you will have to resist the alcoholic devil that brought the problem into your family in the first place. You can't just relax and do nothing.

Judge Drunkenness
By the Company It Keeps

You can always judge something by the company it keeps. Well, when you check out Galatians 5:20-21, you'll find out that drunkenness is listed among the works of the flesh — along with **adultery, envy, strife, witchcraft and idolatry!**

So judge strong drink by the company it keeps. It is definitely an enemy to us. It is a desire of the flesh, just like envy, adultery, strife and witchcraft, and therefore opposed to the desires of the Holy Spirit (Galatians 5:17). Drunkenness is one of the sins that darkness uses to bring people into bondage.

Live Habitually By the Holy Spirit

What should you do with desires that are opposed to God? You crucify those desires as you walk by the spirit (Galatians 5:24,25). Learn to dominate your flesh and make no provision for it (Romans 13:14).

You might as well accept the fact that as long as you walk on this earth, you'll have to deal with the conflict between the flesh and the spirit. Your spirit wants you to go God's way (Galatians 5:17) while the flesh wants to pull you back into the natural. The flesh has to be trained to obey God (see Hebrews 5:12-14).

You can win that conflict day by day. You just have to **Walk in the Spirit, and ye shall not fulfil the lust of the flesh** (Galatians 5:16).

So don't open the door to the devil by allowing strong drink to become your companion. Follow God's wise counsel: **Do not get drunk with wine, for that is debauchery; but ever be filled and stimulated with the [Holy] Spirit** (Ephesians 5:18, AMP). When you stay filled with the New Wine, you won't need the kind that comes in a bottle!

You may live in a world where evil continues to increase, but you have been set free from its sinful ways. And as you live by the wisdom of God, you will *stay* free.

Wisdom for Today

If an alcoholic spirit has harassed your family for generations, take authority over its strategies against you and your children in Jesus' name.

Learn to dominate your flesh and make no provision for it.
Walk in the spirit and you won't fulfill the lust of the flesh.

CHAPTER 24
A Home Filled With Precious Riches

*God wants to fill the chambers of your spiritual and
natural house with precious and pleasant riches.
Your part is to walk in His wisdom and to hold fast
to your faith in Him.*

⁂

Proverbs Chapter 24

1   Be not thou envious against evil men, neither desire to be with them.

2   For their heart studieth destruction, and their lips talk of mischief.

3   Through wisdom is an house builded; and by understanding it is established:

4   And by knowledge shall the chambers be filled with all precious and pleasant riches.

5   A wise man is strong; yea, a man of knowledge increaseth strength.

6   For by wise counsel thou shalt make thy war: and in multitude of counsellors there is safety.

7   Wisdom is too high for a fool: he openeth not his mouth in the gate.

8   He that deviseth to do evil shall be called a mischievous person.

9   The thought of foolishness is sin: and the scorner is an abomination to men.

10   If thou faint in the day of adversity, thy strength is small.

11   If thou forbear to deliver them that are drawn unto death, and those that are ready to be slain;

12   If thou sayest, Behold, we knew it not; doth not he that pondereth the heart consider it? and he that keepeth thy soul, doth not he know it? and shall not he render to every man according to his works?

13   My son, eat thou honey, because it is good; and the honeycomb, which is sweet to thy taste:

14   So shall the knowledge of wisdom be unto thy soul: when thou hast found it, then there shall be a reward, and thy expectation shall not be cut off.

15   Lay not wait, O wicked man, against the dwelling of the righteous; spoil not his resting place:

16   For a just man falleth seven times, and riseth up again: but the wicked shall fall into mischief.

17   Rejoice not when thine enemy falleth, and let not thine heart be glad when he stumbleth:

18   Lest the Lord see it, and it displease him, and he turn away his wrath from him.

19   Fret not thyself because of evil men, neither be thou envious at the wicked;

20   For there shall be no reward to the evil man; the candle of the wicked shall be put out.

21   My son, fear thou the Lord and the king: and meddle not with them that are given to change:

22 For their calamity shall rise suddenly; and who knoweth the ruin of them both?

23 These things also belong to the wise. It is not good to have respect of persons in judgment.

24 He that saith unto the wicked, Thou art righteous; him shall the people curse, nations shall abhor him:

25 But to them that rebuke him shall be delight, and a good blessing shall come upon them.

26 Every man shall kiss his lips that giveth a right answer.

27 Prepare thy work without, and make it fit for thyself in the field; and afterwards build thine house.

28 Be not a witness against thy neighbour without cause; and deceive not with thy lips.

29 Say not, I will do so to him as he hath done to me: I will render to the man according to his work.

30 I went by the field of the slothful, and by the vineyard of the man void of understanding;

31 And, lo, it was all grown over with thorns, and nettles had covered the face thereof, and the stone wall thereof was broken down.

32 Then I saw, and considered it well: I looked upon it, and received instruction.

33 Yet a little sleep, a little slumber, a little folding of the hands to sleep:

34 So shall thy poverty come as one that travelleth; and thy want as an armed man.

Hidden Treasures

꒰⟋꒱

When I read through Proverbs 24, I come across verses that remind me of some spiritual landmarks in my own life where I "fought the good fight of faith" and won.

For instance, this chapter includes what I call my "house scripture" — a key passage that we stood on years ago to receive our first home debt free: **Through skillful and godly Wisdom is a house (a life, a home, a family) built, and by understanding it is established [on a sound and good foundation], and by knowledge shall its chambers [of every area] be filled with all precious and pleasant riches** (vv. 3-4, AMP). Isn't that a marvelous Word from God!

So let's look at some faith principles in Proverbs 24 that will help fill our homes and our lives with God's precious and pleasant riches!

Believing for a Home

By 1968, Ken and I had never owned a home. Actually, we hadn't even rented a home that was really desirable!

This was about the time we began to learn how to apply the Word to our lives. This was also the time we found the scripture that says to **keep out of debt and owe no man anything, except to love one another** (Romans 13:8, AMP). Kenneth and I had already made a commitment to obey God's Word no matter what, so when we saw this verse, we immediately stopped charging any purchases or borrowing money.

Well, the one material thing in this life that I really wanted was a nice home. When I was a little girl I didn't play with dolls much but I did play "house."

In 1968, to buy clothes or to have a car without debt looked impossible for us. But to pay cash for a home? I had never heard of such a thing. My mother and dad never even owned a home of their own and at this time I was in my mid-twenties.

But I found scriptures to build my expectations and to make my stand for a home. And one of the main scriptures I stood on was this passage in Proverbs 24. This verse bought the house and then filled it up!

I'd tell the Lord, "By faith I see both our family and our house built by the wisdom of God! I see the knowledge of God filling every chamber with precious and pleasant riches." When the situation looked impossible, I would hang on to that scripture. The devil would say things like, *You sure can't ever have a new house now. Whoever heard of paying cash for a house? How could you ever get the money?* But I had also found another scripture:

And God is able to make all grace (every favor and earthly blessing) come to you in abundance, so that you may always *and* under all circumstances *and* whatever the need be self-sufficient [possessing enough to require no aid or support and furnished in abundance for every good work and charitable donation] (2 Corinthians 9:8, AMP).

Because of this scripture I could say in faith, "God is able! I don't have to know how He will get our new house. All I have to do is trust that He is able, and He will do it."

For a long time it looked as if there was no way we could ever own a house. Until our decision to "get out and stay out" of debt, we had borrowed money for everything we bought. In the natural, paying cash for a home seemed so impossible.

But I kept confessing, "God is able. I see my house filled with precious riches!" I didn't give up. In the meantime God provided us a good place to live, but it wasn't ours.

Well, it took patience to stand in faith for that house. It didn't happen in a year. It didn't happen in two years. But after six years of growing in the wisdom and knowledge of God, we purchased our first home — with cash!

The first house took six years. The next house (principal residence) took three weeks (1980). At this writing we are preparing to build our dream home. Before the plans were finished, the money was there. GLORY TO GOD — HE IS ABLE!

For over thirty years this home has been prepared by faith in the Word of God and by sowing seed for it with words and money. Harvest time is here!

We didn't go from a little rented house to a dream home in one step. God has, over these thirty years of faith, given us every home we asked for, and we have been so blessed. In the walk of faith you can't despise small beginnings. Through faith and patience you inherit the promises (Hebrews 6:12).

Earlier, I discussed the law of gradual or progressive increase, and that law has been my and Ken's experience. You walk in progressive increase because you walk in progressive revelation. Your faith works according to the Word that *you* understand and live by.

Job's friend told him, **Though your beginning was small, yet your latter end would greatly increase** (Job 8:7, AMP). That is exactly what came to pass. **And the Lord turned the captivity of Job and restored his fortunes, when he prayed for his friends; also the Lord gave Job twice as much as he had before** (Job 42:10, AMP).

I'm convinced that God made this earth exclusively for His children. God has title deed to the earth except for that which He has already given. I believe it is important to Him that His children possess it. Remember that God wanted Israel, His covenant people, to possess the land. That was a major part of His blessing.

He didn't create this earth for the devil and his crowd. He made it for His family. His desire for us is to enjoy His provision and rejoice while we give Him all the glory.

By faith we are to:

1. Ask Him for what we desire according to His Word.

2. Believe we receive it when we pray.

3. Act and talk like our prayers were heard and answered.

Now faith is the assurance (the confirmation, that title deed) of the things [we] hope for, being the proof of things [we] do not see and the conviction of their reality [faith perceiving as real fact what is not revealed to the senses] (Hebrews 11:1, AMP).

Though we started small, now we are able to build according to Isaiah 54:2-3 (AMP). **Enlarge the place of your tent, and let the curtains of your habitations be stretched out; spare not; lengthen your cords and strengthen your stakes, For you will spread abroad to the right hand and to the left; and your offspring will possess the nations and make the desolate cities to be inhabited.**

There are other house scriptures that you can stand on as you believe for the perfect home for your family. God promises that the seed of the righteous **shall be mighty upon earth.... Wealth and riches shall be in his house** (Psalm 112:2-3). He also says that **the tabernacle of the upright shall flourish** (Proverbs 14:11).

I saw two more house promises while working on this book: **Every wise woman builds her house...** (Proverbs 14:1, AMP) and **God places the solitary in families and gives the desolate a home in which to dwell; He leads the prisoners out to prosperity; but the rebellious dwell in a parched land** (Psalm 68:6, AMP). (This is also a great scripture for those in prison who are believing God for their future.) These scriptures will produce a harvest of blessing in your home and in your life as you hold fast to your faith and do what you know to do according to the Word. God will give you a home filled with the love of God and precious treasures.

A Word for Tough Times

Sometimes refusing to faint is a hard thing to do when you're facing difficult circumstances. However, God says **if you faint in the day of adversity, your strength is small** (Proverbs 24:10, AMP).

In other words, we should be able to endure pressures and trials in faith until victory comes. We are to hold fast to the Word of God without wavering until we see our answer manifested in the natural realm. If we can't do that, then our strength is small.

But God's Word says we *can* do it! God promises in Psalm 94:12-13 (AMP) to give us the power not to faint in the day of adversity: **Blessed (happy, fortunate, to be envied) is the man whom You discipline and instruct, O Lord, and teach out of Your law, that You may give him *power to keep himself calm in the days of adversity*, until the [inevitable] pit of corruption is dug for the wicked.**

I have that passage bracketed and marked with stars in my Bible because it's so good!

It takes patience to stay calm through the days of adversity. When pressure comes, when impossibilities loom before you, when you hear discouraging reports — that is *not* the time to faint or cave in. That's when you need to stand on the Word and depend on God's power to keep you calm until victory comes!

Don't Fret About Sinners

In order to stay calm in the day of adversity, you have to heed God's admonition to **fret not because of evildoers, neither be envious of the wicked** (Proverbs 24:19, AMP). Psalm 37:1-3 says the same thing. Don't fret about evildoers, but trust in the Lord and do good.

It will stir up your flesh and make you faint in your faith if you allow yourself to start thinking envious thoughts about sinners. For instance, at one time or another you may have thought, *Lord, just look at those heathen people. They live like animals, yet they have so much.*

Well, those people may have material possessions. But if they don't know God, they don't have peace and joy. So they can't truly enjoy even the material things they do possess.

Really, evildoers don't have anything for you to envy. They may look good; it may seem as if they're having a good time. But if they don't belong to God's family, they aren't happy inside there is no peace outside of God. God says that there is no peace for the wicked (Isaiah 57:21).

Sometimes believers not only fret against evildoers, but they fret against the Lord because they think sinners are more blessed than they are — and they don't like it! When people fret against the Lord, God tells them, **Your words have been stout against me** (Malachi 3:13).

The Bible explains what kind of words God considers to be "stout" against Him: **Ye have said, It is vain to serve God: and what profit is it that we have kept his ordinance...? And now we call the proud happy...yea, they that tempt God are even delivered** (Malachi 3:14-15).

God doesn't appreciate your chiding Him for treating someone else better than you think He has treated you. That's not trust! So when you ask God, "What good is it to serve You?" He says, "Those words are stout against Me."

Then Malachi 3:16 (AMP) shows us the way we *should* act toward the Lord: **Those who feared the Lord talked often one to another; and the Lord listened and heard it, and a book of remembrance was written before Him of those who reverenced and worshipfully feared the Lord and who thought on His name.**

You see, the Lord hears us when we talk to one another. He doesn't just hear us in church. He is with us all the time. He hears stout words against Himself when we murmur and complain, or He hears words of reverence and worship.

Not only that, but God remembers what He hears. He never forgets to reward you when you walk in honor of Him and hold fast to your confession of faith in His ability and goodness. Your part is to keep walking in God's wisdom — what He says is right. God's commitment is to fill the chambers of your spiritual and natural house with precious and pleasant riches!

Wisdom for Today

❧

Whatever you're believing God for that's in line with the Word, faithfully confess, "God is able to bring it to pass!"

Refuse to faint or grow weary in well-doing when you face difficult circumstances.

When pressure comes, stand on the Word and keep calm until victory comes!

CHAPTER 25
Rule Your Spirit With the Word

The storms of life need never catch you unprepared.
As you become rooted in God's Word, you can
maintain calm, steady control over your spirit
in the face of any adversity.

❦

Proverbs Chapter 25

1 These are also proverbs of Solomon, which the men of Hezekiah king of Judah copied out.

2 It is the glory of God to conceal a thing: but the honour of kings is to search out a matter.

3 The heaven for height, and the earth for depth, and the heart of kings is unsearchable.

4 Take away the dross from the silver, and there shall come forth a vessel for the finer.

5 Take away the wicked from before the king, and his throne shall be established in righteousness.

6 Put not forth thyself in the presence of the king, and stand not in the place of great men:

7 For better it is that it be said unto thee, Come up hither; than that thou shouldest be put lower in the presence of the prince whom thine eyes have seen.

8 Go not forth hastily to strive, lest thou know not what to do in the end thereof, when thy neighbour hath put thee to shame.

9 Debate thy cause with thy neighbour himself; and discover not a secret to another:

10 Lest he that heareth it put thee to shame, and thine infamy turn not away.

11 A word fitly spoken is like apples of gold in pictures of silver.

12 As an earring of gold, and an ornament of fine gold, so is a wise reprover upon an obedient ear.

13 As the cold of snow in the time of harvest, so is a faithful messenger to them that send him: for he refresheth the soul of his masters.

14 Whoso boasteth himself of a false gift is like clouds and wind without rain.

15 By long forbearing is a prince persuaded, and a soft tongue breaketh the bone.

16 Hast thou found honey? eat so much as is sufficient for thee, lest thou be filled therewith, and vomit it.

17 Withdraw thy foot from thy neighbour's house; lest he be weary of thee, and so hate thee.

18 A man that beareth false witness against his neighbour is a maul, and a sword, and a sharp arrow.

19 Confidence in an unfaithful man in time of trouble is like a broken tooth, and a foot out of joint.

20 As he that taketh away a garment in cold weather, and as vinegar upon nitre, so is he that singeth songs to an heavy heart.

21 If thine enemy be hungry, give him bread to eat; and if he be thirsty, give him water to drink:

22 For thou shalt heap coals of fire upon his head, and the Lord shall reward thee.

23 The north wind driveth away rain: so doth an angry countenance a backbiting tongue.

24 It is better to dwell in the corner of the housetop, than with a brawling woman and in a wide house.

25 As cold waters to a thirsty soul, so is good news from a far country.

26 A righteous man falling down before the wicked is as a troubled fountain, and a corrupt spring.

27 It is not good to eat much honey: so for men to search their own glory is not glory.

28 He that hath no rule over his own spirit is like a city that is broken down, and without walls.

Hidden Treasures

The last verse of Proverbs 25 talks about the theme I want to focus on in our discussion of this chapter: how to rule your spirit by the Word of God. This is such an important issue in your walk with God that it's worth taking some extra time to talk about it. You see, if you don't rule yourself, you are defenseless against the strategies of the enemy.

Rule Your Spirit
By Renewing Your Mind

A person who doesn't submit himself to God is vulnerable to his flesh, his emotions, circumstances and the devil. **He who has no rule over his own spirit is like a city that is broken down and without walls** (Proverbs 25:28, AMP). His walls of defense are down. He continually responds to the pressures of life in the wrong way and only increases his own trouble. But no matter how undisciplined a person is, he can regain rule over his entire being by renewing his mind with the Word of God enough to do it. When the spirit (the reborn man on the inside) rises up in obedience to God's Word, the flesh has to obey.

You see, God wants to give us such a great measure of steadiness that in the face of any adversity, we can still maintain calm, steady control over our actions. That's what it means to have rule over our spirit.

But it requires cooperation on our part. God doesn't just give us those qualities automatically; we have to renew our minds with His Word. As we do, we become more and more stable. We start gaining control over our thought life and our emotions.

I have seen the most unstable people transformed by God's Word. I've even watched the transformation of some who at one time were on the verge of suicide and had to be watched constantly because of their mental or emotional instability.

These people began to deposit the Word into their hearts on a regular basis and their thoughts began to conform to God's way of thinking.

By faithfully staying in God's Word, they were transformed into stable, steady people that could be depended on — because they took time to renew their minds with the Word. In other words, they got their thoughts in agreement with God's thoughts and their talk in agreement with God's talk.

It doesn't have to take long. How long depends on how diligent you are to make the transformation. Proverbs 4 is the formula: Word going in your ears + Word in front of your eyes = Word in the midst of your heart!

So it doesn't really matter what you're like in the natural. You may be calm or unpredictable, steady or unsteady, and the results will still be the same. If you keep sowing God's Word into your spirit, eventually it *will* renew your mind and cause your spirit to gain control of your actions.

Insights Into Renewing Your Mind

Vine's defines "renewing your mind" as *the adjustment of the moral and spiritual vision and thinking to the mind of God.*[1] Someone else said that "renewing" means *the gradual conforming of the man more and more to that new spiritual world into which he has been introduced and in which he now lives and moves.*

The process of renewing your mind takes place in your soul, which includes your mind, will and emotions. When you were born again, your spirit

---

[1] W. E. Vine, *Vine's Complete Expository Dictionary of Old and New Testament Words* (Nashville: Thomas Nelson Publishers, 1996), p. 524.

became instantly recreated, changed to the image of God. However, your body stayed the same, and your soul still had to be renewed by the Word of God.

So you *are* saved in your spirit; you *are being* saved in your soul; and you *will be* ultimately saved in your body on that great day of resurrection when your physical body becomes immortal. Until that day, you *are* saved from sickness and disease in the body.

Steady in the Midst of the Storm

When you delight in the Word, renewing your mind with its truth, you become like a tree planted by the water ready to bring forth fruit (Psalm 1:3). The storms of life will never catch you unprepared. The winds may blow, and the rain may pour down, but you will stay steady in the midst of it all.

You see, it's easy to delight in the Word once you receive the revelation that "This Word belongs to *me* and it is full of wonderful blessings. I have what it says I have. I am what it says I am. I can do what it says I can do, because *God* said it." When you begin to think and talk like that, you become a tree that is ready to bring forth fruit. Your roots are deep and your thought patterns changed to conform to God's Word.

But the soulish part of you must be trained. It must be made whole and sound by growing in the knowledge of God's Word. That training and renewing process is what makes you stable in the midst of any circumstance you face.

You may be the type of person who is liable to throw a fit of anger at any time. You may have been that way all of your life. Well, the way to be set free from that carnal behavior is to feed your spirit and your mind on the Word of God.

As you do, the Word will affect your spirit, causing it to become stronger. It will affect your will, your thoughts and your emotions, causing them to agree with the Word. You will start gaining control of your anger and frustration — or any other sinful tendency that tries to overtake you.

The truth is, it doesn't matter what a person was before he was born again. He could have been a con artist, a thief or even a murderer. But after he's born again and his mind becomes renewed by God's Word, his thought patterns will change. He'll begin to think right things. He will gain rule over his entire being, causing Proverbs 16:32 to come to pass in his life: **He that is slow to** anger is better than the mighty; and he that ruleth his spirit than he that taketh a city.

So don't be like a **city that is broken down and without walls** (Proverbs 25:28, AMP). Remember, there is an enemy out there that looks for broken-down walls and open doors through which he can enter and destroy the lives of those who will let him have control.

Create a lifestyle of feeding your spirit and soul the revelation of God's will for you from His Word. Be willing to make changes as you see what God says is right. This is the wise way to avoid making mistakes that set into motion consequences that can cause you trouble for the rest of your life.

Overindulging in Pleasure

Here's another principle that will help you maintain control over your spirit: *Enjoy only as much natural pleasure in this life as you can spiritually afford*: **Have you found [pleasure sweet like] honey? Eat only as much as is sufficient for you, lest, being filled with it, you vomit it** (v. 16, AMP).

In other words, this verse is saying, "Don't overindulge in pleasure."

You know, we can have a good time in this life, taking pleasure in wholesome, enjoyable activities. But we can't live for pleasure. We can't give natural pleasure a place in our lives that it doesn't deserve.

It's possible to go after entertainment and pleasure in this life until you don't have any time left for your relationship with God. That's a good way to lose the rule over your spirit, soul and body. Remember, Jesus said that the pleasures of this world can choke the Word and make it fruitless (Mark 4:19).

If you're born again and Spirit-filled, you know when you do wrong. You know when God is trying to separate you from something that is hindering your walk with Him.

It may be that you're giving too much time and attention to something that isn't wrong in itself, but it's just wasting your time. You know in your spirit that God is asking you to spend more time building your spiritual life and less time pursuing that area of your natural life.

God may ask you to separate yourself from some of these pleasures if they're hindering your walk with Him. For example, when you come home at night, you don't want to study the Word, listen to a teaching tape or spend time in prayer. Instead, night after night you focus your attention on your favorite activity or hobby that may not be sin but is stealing too much time away from God.

So pay attention to that tug in your heart. Answer His call and set aside activities that keep you from spending the time in His Word and in His presence that is necessary to live a life of victory.

God wants you to go on in Him and fulfill His wonderful plan for your life. But you can only do that as you maintain the rule over your spirit, soul and body!

Wisdom for Today

Get your thoughts in agreement with God's thoughts — feed your spirit and mind on the Word of God.

Receive the revelation: God's Word belongs to you. You can have what it says you have. You are what it says you are. You can do what it says you can do.

Enjoy only as much natural pleasure in your life as you can spiritually afford.

CHAPTER 26
Avoid the Way of the Fool

You're called to walk in the heavenly places with God.
Don't sacrifice a life lived to His glory and power just to
follow the ways of the fool!

⁂

Proverbs Chapter 26

1 As snow in summer, and as rain in harvest, so honour is not seemly for a fool.

2 As the bird by wandering, as the swallow by flying, so the curse causeless shall not come.

3 A whip for the horse, a bridle for the ass, and a rod for the fool's back.

4 Answer not a fool according to his folly, lest thou also be like unto him.

5 Answer a fool according to his folly, lest he be wise in his own conceit.

6 He that sendeth a message by the hand of a fool cutteth off the feet, and drinketh damage.

7 The legs of the lame are not equal: so is a parable in the mouth of fools.

8 As he that bindeth a stone in a sling, so is he that giveth honour to a fool.

9 As a thorn goeth up into the hand of a drunkard, so is a parable in the mouth of fools.

10 The great God that formed all things both rewardeth the fool, and rewardeth transgressors.

11 As a dog returneth to his vomit, so a fool returneth to his folly.

12 Seest thou a man wise in his own conceit? there is more hope of a fool than of him.

13 The slothful man saith, There is a lion in the way; a lion is in the streets.

14 As the door turneth upon his hinges, so doth the slothful upon his bed.

15 The slothful hideth his hand in his bosom; it grieveth him to bring it again to his mouth.

16 The sluggard is wiser in his own conceit than seven men that can render a reason.

17 He that passeth by, and meddleth with strife belonging not to him, is like one that taketh a dog by the ears.

18 As a mad man who casteth firebrands, arrows, and death,

19 So is the man that deceiveth his neighbour, and saith, Am not I in sport?

20 Where no wood is, there the fire goeth out: so where there is no talebearer, the strife ceaseth.

21 As coals are to burning coals, and wood to fire; so is a contentious man to kindle strife.

22 The words of a talebearer are as wounds, and they go down into the innermost parts of the belly.

23 Burning lips and a wicked heart are like a potsherd covered with silver dross.

24 He that hateth dissembleth with his lips, and layeth up deceit within him;

25 When he speaketh fair, believe him not: for there are seven abominations in his heart.

26 Whose hatred is covered by deceit, his wickedness shall be shewed before the whole congregation.

27 Whoso diggeth a pit shall fall therein: and he that rolleth a stone, it will return upon him.

28 A lying tongue hateth those that are afflicted by it; and a flattering mouth worketh ruin.

Hidden Treasures

God makes it very clear in the book of Proverbs that the way of the fool is the way to avoid. In Proverbs 26, He tells us some of the fool's ways to steer clear of as we walk through life on this earth.

Never Overestimate Yourself

Proverbs 26:1-11 gives a long list of reasons why the way of a fool is hopeless. Then verse 12 (AMP) asks, **Do you see a man wise in his own eyes and conceit? There is more hope for a [self-confident] fool than for him.** That's really saying something, because there isn't much hope for a fool who won't heed correction!

The truth is, you're acting like a self-confident fool when you are wise in your own conceits. That's disobeying God's admonition to **live in harmony with one another; do not be haughty (snobbish, high-minded, exclusive).... Never overestimate yourself or be wise in your own conceits** (Romans 12:16, AMP). And disobeying God *is* the way of the fool.

Don't Be a Sluggard

The way of the sluggard is another foolish path to avoid: **The sluggard says, There is a lion in the way! A lion is in the streets! As the door turns on its hinges, so does the lazy man [move not from his place] upon his bed** (Proverbs 26:13-14, AMP).

In other words, the sluggard hears that danger is nearby, but he doesn't do one thing to avoid that danger. He hears about a lion in the street, but he's so lazy he doesn't even move. The sluggard is the ancient version of a "couch potato"!

This passage about the sluggard reminds me of Proverbs 27:12 (AMP): **A prudent man sees the evil and hides himself, but the simple pass on and are punished [with suffering].** People who are too spiritually lazy to separate themselves from the dangers and evils of this world are going to suffer consequences.

So don't hang out with those the Bible calls "fools" or "the simple" — those who ignore the dangers of indulging in sin and then suffer the consequences. See the evil, and hide from it!

Don't Feed on the World's Sin

Minister the gospel to the unrighteous, but don't "hang out" with them unless it's on your level and in your surroundings, because they'll start influencing you toward their unholy way of thinking. Soon you'll be watching the same television shows and movies they watch, feeding your mind on things that are full of sin.

You and I don't have any business feeding on the world's sin. We've been set apart for God and His sacred use! We shouldn't watch situation comedies on television that make light of immorality and dishonor God. Programs like that are intended to desensitize people to sin. They applaud evil.

I realize that people will argue about that. They'll say, "It's just a little harmless fun — it's nothing serious."

The Bible warns us about that foolish attitude. It says not to be like the children of Israel who indulged in sinful, worldly ways and **sat down to eat and drink, and rose up to play** (1 Corinthians 10:7).

Don't play around with sin the way worldly people do. They are going the way of the fool.

Compromising your spiritual walk for something as silly as a fleshly indulgence is simply foolish. It doesn't make sense to hold on to the world's garbage when you can walk in heavenly places in Christ (Ephesians 1:3). Don't let fleshly pleasures hinder you when you can live in the glory of God!

191

Conformed to Jesus, Not the World

We need to keep in mind who we are in the eyes of God. He asks us, **What fellowship hath righteousness with unrighteousness? and what communion hath light with darkness?** (2 Corinthians 6:14).

Those are good questions. We've been made the righteousness of God and are indwelt by the very Spirit of God Himself. So what fellowship *do* we have with the activities of this world that dishonor God? The answer is *none*, because **God hath not called us unto uncleanness, but unto holiness** (1 Thessalonians 4:7).

God couldn't get any plainer than that. He's called us unto holiness. He's called us not to be conformed to this world (Romans 12:2), but to be separate from it.

You see, the world tries to squeeze us into its mold. And when we break out of its mold, the world makes fun of us and persecutes us, calling us "holy rollers" or religious fanatics.

Satan is the one who entices us to be like the world because he is the father of this world system that operates in the darkness. He's always trying to bombard us, trying to make us think like he thinks and talk like he talks. He wants us to use negative words that rob and destroy everything good in our lives.

So what *are* we supposed to conform to? To the image of Jesus:

For whom he did foreknow, he also did predestinate to be conformed to the image of his Son, that he might be the firstborn among many brethren (Romans 8:29).

You know, we are just passing through this life. It is not even a snap of the fingers compared to eternity. This is just our training ground where we learn to give God glory in a natural body.

We'll never be able to serve God in just the same way we can right now. Yes, we'll always serve Him and give Him glory throughout eternity. But when we get to heaven, we'll only have a choice between good and good.

Here on earth we have a choice between good and evil. We can stand for God. We can be faithful in this world even under pressure. This gives God glory. We can prove the good, acceptable and perfect will of God as we live in His ways of wisdom (Romans 12:2).

Or we can choose to go the way of the fool. We can conform to the world's thinking and be sick, broke, fearful and without any answers to life.

When believers try to live in the foolish ways of the world, they put themselves in danger. In compromising themselves, they give the devil a foothold in their lives (Ephesians 4:27, AMP).

That's why there's weak faith in Christian circles, even among those who call themselves "people of faith." Many believers know what the Word says, but fail to act out their faith because they aren't separated from the world the way they should be. They aren't separated unto God and the work He's called them to do.

I am convinced that the more we give ourselves to God, the more He will manifest His power and glory in our midst. I want to see that glorious manifestation. I want it badly enough to give God my best effort in being faithful to Him and what He calls me to do.

I believe we can all be more separated from the spirit of the world. We never need to fellowship with darkness. We can and we must avoid the ways of the fool!

Wisdom for Today

Minister to the unrighteous, but don't fellowship on their level.

Don't feed on the world's sin that makes light
of immorality and dishonors God.

Glorify God in your earthly body — choose good instead of evil.

CHAPTER 27
The Faithfulness of the Wise

Faithfulness is the spiritual force issuing out of your spirit that causes you to increase and abound in the blessings of God.

❦

Proverbs Chapter 27

1 Boast not thyself of to morrow; for thou knowest not what a day may bring forth.

2 Let another man praise thee, and not thine own mouth; a stranger, and not thine own lips.

3 A stone is heavy, and the sand weighty; but a fool's wrath is heavier than them both.

4 Wrath is cruel, and anger is outrageous; but who is able to stand before envy?

5 Open rebuke is better than secret love.

6 Faithful are the wounds of a friend; but the kisses of an enemy are deceitful.

7 The full soul loatheth an honeycomb; but to the hungry soul every bitter thing is sweet.

8 As a bird that wandereth from her nest, so is a man that wandereth from his place.

9 Ointment and perfume rejoice the heart: so doth the sweetness of a man's friend by hearty counsel.

10 Thine own friend, and thy father's friend, forsake not; neither go into thy brother's house in the day of thy calamity: for better is a neighbour that is near than a brother far off.

11 My son, be wise, and make my heart glad, that I may answer him that reproacheth me.

12 A prudent man foreseeth the evil, and hideth himself; but the simple pass on, and are punished.

13 Take his garment that is surety for a stranger, and take a pledge of him for a strange woman.

14 He that blesseth his friend with a loud voice, rising early in the morning, it shall be counted a curse to him.

15 A continual dropping in a very rainy day and a contentious woman are alike.

16 Whosoever hideth her hideth the wind, and the ointment of his right hand, which betrayeth itself.

17 Iron sharpeneth iron; so a man sharpeneth the countenance of his friend.

18 Whoso keepeth the fig tree shall eat the fruit thereof: so he that waiteth on his master shall be honoured.

19 As in water face answereth to face, so the heart of man to man.

20 Hell and destruction are never full; so the eyes of man are never satisfied.

21   As the fining pot for silver, and the furnace for gold; so is a man to his praise.

22   Though thou shouldest bray a fool in a mortar among wheat with a pestle, yet will not his foolishness depart from him.

23   Be thou diligent to know the state of thy flocks, and look well to thy herds.

24   For riches are not for ever: and doth the crown endure to every generation?

25   The hay appeareth, and the tender grass showeth itself, and herbs of the mountains are gathered.

26   The lambs are for thy clothing, and the goats are the price of the field.

27   And thou shalt have goats' milk enough for thy food, for the food of thy household, and for the maintenance for thy maidens.

Hidden Treasures

Prosperity in God is only possible as you walk in His way of faithfulness. Faithfulness is a fruit of the spirit — a force that directly opens the door to God in every area of your life — spiritual, physical and mental.

Faithfulness is absolutely crucial not only in your walk with God, but on the job, in your relationships and in every other area of life. So as we look at Chapter 27, let's talk about this godly force that was imparted into your new nature to help you succeed in life.

The Faithfulness of a Friend

To be faithful means to be trustworthy and dependable. The dictionary says that a faithful man is one who firmly adheres to duty. He possesses true fidelity. He is loyal, true to allegiance and constant in the performance of duties or services.

Think of that definition in relation to Proverbs 27:6 (AMP): **Faithful are the wounds of a friend, but the kisses of an enemy are lavish and deceitful.**

Loyal, faithful friends whose **open rebuke is better than love that is hidden** are a true blessing of God (v. 5, AMP). Those are the kind of friends Ken and I have. They are godly people who act the same all the time, whether they're at church or at home. We ride motorcycles together, and although we might look like the world wearing our helmets and leathers, we have a grand time praising God and talking faith together during our rides — just as we do when we're preaching together at conventions.

True friends are faithful to tell us the truth and give us God's wisdom when we share our hearts with them. They are the kind of friends Proverbs 27:9 (AMP) talks about: **Oil and perfume rejoice the heart; so does the sweetness of a friend's counsel that comes from the heart.**

Someone who really loves you will tell you the truth. He tells you what will help you, even if it sometimes hurts to hear it. On the other hand, someone who doesn't care much about you and isn't as concerned for your welfare may just flatter you or say what he thinks you want to hear.

That's why we should be wise enough to appreciate our friends who are faithful to tell us the truth and give us wise counsel from God's Word. Faithful counsel can be a "wound" that works for our good!

Faithfulness in Our Spiritual Walk

The spiritual force of faithfulness helps us, first of all, in our relationship with God. Faithfulness keeps us doing what God considers right and helps us choose to act on His Word.

As you are faithful to store the Word of God in your heart in any area of your life, the Word can change and renew the spirit of your mind to think like God. Just stay willing to receive His correction, and God will keep you right on course. Then as you act on God's Word, you will enjoy the fruit of your faithfulness.

The Reward of Faithfulness

In Matthew 25:14-30, Jesus told the parable of the talents. In this parable, a man gave talents to his servants. To one servant, the man gave five talents; to another, two; and to another, one. Then he went on a long journey.

When the man returned, the one with five talents brought him five more, and the one with two brought him two more. So he said to each servant, "Well done, good and faithful servant. You have been faithful over a few things, so I will make you ruler over many things" (Matthew 25:21,23, author's paraphrase).

Both of these servants did well. They were faithful, and as a result, they increased. This parable teaches us that faithfulness brings increase.

But the servant who had been given one talent brought back only that one talent. Because he was afraid, he didn't do anything with the talent given him.

(Read closely, and you'll see that servant was full of fear because he didn't trust the man who gave him the talent.) What happened to that one talent when he wasn't faithful with it? It was taken from him and given to the one who had five.

You may say, "But that isn't fair; that servant already *had* five!" Yes, but he knew what to do with the five talents he'd been given — he'd already doubled them to ten. That meant he also knew what to do with the ten talents he now had, so he was given one more. That's the reward of faithfulness.

The faithful servants were told, "You have been faithful over a few things, so I will make you ruler over many things." The faithful will be blessed with more, but the unfaithful will lose what they have. Jesus repeated this same principle, saying, **For to him who has will more be given; and from him who has nothing, even what he has will be taken away [by force]** (Mark 4:25, AMP).

I want to stand before Jesus one day and hear Him say: "Well done, good and faithful servant!" I get excited just thinking about that day. It's coming. I believe He's coming soon. I believe this is the "last generation." But, one thing I know for sure, it's my last generation! So I'm going to live like it and to God be all the Glory!

Increase and Promotion

Faithfulness in life not only works when you are faithful toward God, but it also works when you are faithful toward others, such as your employer or employees. Proverbs 27:18 (AMP) says, **Whoever tends the fig tree shall eat its fruit; so he who patiently and faithfully guards and heeds his master shall be honored.**

I want to look for a moment at what you are doing today to earn a living. Maybe you work at a job you don't really enjoy. Maybe you don't think it's an important job.

Even if you aren't satisfied with your job, in God's eyes it's still important how you perform your duties. I'm going to give you a little clue that will work for you: **A faithful man shall *abound* with blessings** (Proverbs 28:20, AMP). One thing that verse means is this: A faithful man will be *promoted*.

Therefore, whatever your job may be — even if it's just menial labor you think is terrible — you should do the best job you can, and God will promote you. That's the principle of increase this verse promises.

You have to be faithful where you are. Do your work as unto the Lord, and He will reward you. If you work for someone else, faithfulness will cause you to increase and be promoted. And if you run your own business, your faithfulness to operate it according to the Word will bring you increase. In either case, you will abound with blessings as you are faithful!

Honesty on the Job

Faithfulness in the workplace is absolutely essential in order to increase on the job. Jesus said, **He who is faithful in a very little [thing] is faithful also in much** (Luke 16:10, AMP).

Jesus was talking about being both faithful and honest, especially when performing your responsibilities at your job. You might think, *Surely Christian people don't need to be told to do that.* But they do!

For example, from the beginning of this ministry even until recently we have had to deal with Christians who work in our office and steal. It's hard for me to believe too, but people who haven't established a strong foundation in their lives of God's ways of doing and being right, aren't strong in resisting temptation.

How could a Christian who knows better get into a situation like that? He might think, *I'll just borrow this money for two weeks; then I'll put it back.* But you can't "borrow" money that doesn't belong to you without permission. That is not borrowing. That is stealing.

A basic principle of God states, **Thou shalt not steal** (Exodus 20:15). You can't be blessed when you steal. God considers stealing serious enough to put it in the TOP TEN!

The devil is crazy and he'll try to talk you into doing something crazy. (Notice, I did not say "he will make you." The devil can't make you do anything. He has to persuade you to agree with him. That is called a temptation. The moment you have an evil thought, speak "in the name of Jesus" and rebuke it. Refuse to accept it into your mind.)

Perhaps you want to be promoted on the job, but you spend time chatting with co-workers or using company time to make personal telephone calls when you should be working. That means you are stealing time from your employer, and that's dishonest. And if you are dishonest in a little, you will be dishonest in a lot.

Unfaithful practices like these will keep you from prospering. Now, doing these things may seem all right to you. You may even have made excuses for being dishonest in little ways. Or maybe you have never even thought about whether these practices are right or wrong.

That's why it is so important to continually feed on the Word of God. The Word discerns your thoughts and the intents of your heart. It teaches you what is right and how to live honorably.

You are not to serve your employer just because he is watching over you. You should serve him because it's the *right* thing to do, the *honest* thing to do, the *faithful* thing to do.

Let's say you start a new job, and it only takes a day or two to see that other people on the job aren't doing what's right. Some may be goofing off, talking on the phone or just disappearing a few hours every day when no one notices. Before long, you start to think, *Well, I guess I can do that too.*

But you *can't* do that too — not if you are a Christian. As a believer, you must be faithful, regardless of what those around you are doing.

Your faithfulness in the workplace will cause you to receive answers to problems because you are tied into the wisdom of God. You will have an answer for that company when no one else knows what to do, and that kind of wisdom brings promotion.

I'm talking about being a bright light in a dark world. But you won't be a bright light if you act just like those who are living in darkness. As Luke 16:12 says, **If ye have not been faithful in that which is another man's, who shall give you that which is your own?**

This principle also applies when you use your employer's equipment on the job. For instance, you may drive a company truck. Well, if you treat that truck badly just because it's not yours, you are not a candidate for receiving your own truck. If you don't take care of someone else's vehicle, how can you qualify to have a good vehicle of your own?

Even if you get one, somebody will mistreat it. Jesus said to do unto others as we would have them do unto us (Luke 6:31).

Always Do Your Best

So it's extremely important how faithful you are on your job, whatever that job may be. For instance, if you work in a hotel making beds, your beds should be the best-made beds in the hotel!

If you work for minimum wage, don't just work, thinking, *This job is the pits. I don't like it, so I'll just do the least I can today to get by.* That kind of attitude will make you miserable all day long. Instead, you should work throughout the day thinking, *I'm going to walk in the love of God on this job today and do the best I can.*

No matter what your job, determine to be a blessing every day. If you work as a waitress, determine, *I'm just going to love God all day long and be kind to the people I serve. I will be a blessing today.* Every time you serve a cup of coffee, say to yourself, *I'm doing this as unto the Lord.* Then smile at your customers and make them feel good. You could end up managing that restaurant! We know for sure your tips will be great! That's just the way faithfulness works.

Do Your Job as Unto the Lord

The character quality of diligence is closely tied to the force of faithfulness. Faithfulness causes you to be diligent. Even if you don't like working at your present job, sow a seed by diligently doing a good job right where you are. Proverbs 27:23 (AMP) says, **Be diligent to know the state of your flocks, and look well to your herds.**

As you diligently work, you will be a candidate for promotion because promotion comes from the Lord (Psalm 75:6-7).

By doing your best work as unto the Lord, you are sowing a seed for your future. Tell God: "Lord, this is my job, so I will walk in Your joy. I'll do a good job making those beds. I'll clean to the best of my ability to Your glory, Lord. I'm sowing this work as seed for my new job, and I'm believing for the best job I've ever had!"

Now, this attitude helps you be promoted. Besides, it will give you a much better day! Instead of being angry inside about your job — whether it's making beds, waiting tables or ditchdigging — you can rejoice because you're planting seed!

Faithfulness positions you to be blessed, because you're following God's instructions: **Whatever may be your task, work at it heartily (from the soul), as [something done] for the Lord and not for men** (Colossians 3:23, AMP).

If you will apply this scripture to your life, it will work peace and increase in your life, whether you work for yourself or for someone else.

So begin to release the force of faithfulness in your life. Judge yourself in every situation: *Am I being faithful?* Make the force of faithfulness a lifestyle. Faithfulness is a fruit of the spirit. It is an issue of life that is part of your new nature and it's powerful. Be faithful even in the little things — and then expect to *abound* in blessings!

Wisdom for Today

Be faithful to spend time in the Word. Don't ever get too busy for God.

Everything you do, do it unto the Lord. If you don't like your present job, sow seeds of diligence for a better one!

Judge yourself in every situation: Is this the faithful thing to do?

CHAPTER 28
Guard the Ways of Justice

We are to become God's voice on the earth, guarding
the ways of justice in a very imperfect world. As we do,
He will cause us to dwell securely in the land.

Proverbs Chapter 28

1   The wicked flee when no man pursueth: but the righteous are bold as a lion.

2   For the transgression of a land many are the princes thereof: but by a man of understanding and knowledge the state thereof shall be prolonged.

3   A poor man that oppresseth the poor is like a sweeping rain which leaveth no food.

4   They that forsake the law praise the wicked: but such as keep the law contend with them.

5   Evil men understand not judgment: but they that seek the Lord understand all things.

6   Better is the poor that walketh in his uprightness, than he that is perverse in his ways, though he be rich.

7   Whoso keepeth the law is a wise son: but he that is a companion of riotous men shameth his father.

8   He that by usury and unjust gain increaseth his substance, he shall gather it for him that will pity the poor.

9   He that turneth away his ear from hearing the law, even his prayer shall be abomination.

10   Whoso causeth the righteous to go astray in an evil way, he shall fall himself into his own pit: but the upright shall have good things in possession.

11   The rich man is wise in his own conceit; but the poor that hath understanding searcheth him out.

12   When righteous men do rejoice, there is great glory: but when the wicked rise, a man is hidden.

13   He that covereth his sins shall not prosper: but whoso confesseth and forsaketh them shall have mercy.

14   Happy is the man that feareth alway: but he that hardeneth his heart shall fall into mischief.

15   As a roaring lion, and a ranging bear; so is a wicked ruler over the poor people.

16   The prince that wanteth understanding is also a great oppressor: but he that hateth covetousness shall prolong his days.

17   A man that doeth violence to the blood of any person shall flee to the pit; let no man stay him.

18   Whoso walketh uprightly shall be saved: but he that is perverse in his ways shall fall at once.

19 He that tilleth his land shall have plenty of bread: but he that followeth after vain persons shall have poverty enough.

20 A faithful man shall abound with blessings: but he that maketh haste to be rich shall not be innocent.

21 To have respect of persons is not good: for for a piece of bread that man will transgress.

22 He that hasteth to be rich hath an evil eye, and considereth not that poverty shall come upon him.

23 He that rebuketh a man afterwards shall find more favour than he that flattereth with the tongue.

24 Whoso robbeth his father or his mother, and saith, It is no transgression; the same is the companion of a destroyer.

25 He that is of a proud heart stirreth up strife: but he that putteth his trust in the Lord shall be made fat.

26 He that trusteth in his own heart is a fool: but whoso walketh wisely, he shall be delivered.

27 He that giveth unto the poor shall not lack: but he that hideth his eyes shall have many a curse.

28 When the wicked rise, men hide themselves: but when they perish, the righteous increase.

Hidden Treasures

Proverbs 28 has much to say about preserving God's ways of justice in the midst of man's injustice to man. God is a God of justice, and He wants us to be people of justice in a world where too few care enough anymore to stand for truth, integrity and honor.

Evil Men Don't Understand Justice

Satan is the god of this world, in that the world follows him and allows him to rule them in darkness. Those who belong to his kingdom of darkness don't see and understand the value of walking in righteousness and justice. Their inner man is spiritually dead, so they don't have the heart for it either.

Light comes to us as we hear the truth. Jesus said that if at any time a man would hear and understand and be converted (be turned to the Lord) he would be healed (Matthew 13:15). That's why **evil men do not understand justice, but they who crave and seek the Lord understand it fully** (Proverbs 28:5, AMP).

So it shouldn't surprise us when evil men say that something is right, and we know from God's Word that it's wrong. We shouldn't even expect the world to understand God's ways of righteous judgment. What looks right to the sinner is *not* right to God.

Many times we hear people in authority say something in a speech or on the news, and we think, *Where in the world did they come up with that idea? How could they think that what they are proposing is right to do?*

They think that way because they are darkened in their spirit and mind. They are alienated from the only One from Whom they can find words of wisdom that have **nothing contrary to truth or crooked in them** (Proverbs 8:8, AMP).

The Bible reveals God as a God of justice Who **[earnestly] waits [expecting, looking, and longing] to be gracious to you** (Isaiah 30:18, AMP). So in order to walk in God's ways of wisdom, you must be a person of justice.

Unjust Gain Gathered
For the Just

Proverbs 28:8 (AMP) talks about one form of injustice that God will make right Himself: **He who by charging excessive interest and who by unjust efforts to get gain increases his material possession gathers it for him [to spend] who is kind and generous to the poor.**

Can you imagine how much money in this day and time has been gathered by usury, or excessive interest and unjust gain? I mean, consider how much drug money criminals can't even spend — money buried in boxes in the ground and hidden under beds. This scripture is talking about huge amounts of money! And even if it has been "laundered," turned into so-called "legitimate" money and invested in stocks or real estate, God — The Judge — knows its origin. And all that money is being gathered for the people who will have pity on the poor.

The Bible is telling us God will take care of the transfer to those who do right. In other words, it is not righteous for thieves, murderers, drug dealers, whoremongers, loan sharks, pornographers, and such, to have the wealth of *His* earth. God is saying, "I'll take care of it and I'll put it where it will do some good!"

Be a person who shows kindness to the poor, so you can qualify for the transfer. God will make straight that crooked path of injustice and bless you in the process!

For God giveth to a man that is good in his sight wisdom, and knowledge, and joy: but to the sinner he giveth travail, to gather and to heap up, that he may give to him that is good before God (Ecclesiastes 2:26).

Pray for Your Leaders

I'll tell you one of the most important ways you can help guard the ways of justice: pray for God to give us righteous leaders. We must have leaders of integrity who care for God and this nation more than they care for themselves.

You should be interceding for your nation and its leaders every day, believing and thanking God for righteous, godly people in authority in the land. We need men and women in office who will listen to God and do what He says, because **when the [uncompromisingly] righteous triumph, there is great glory and celebration; but when the wicked rise [to power], men hide themselves** (Proverbs 28:12, AMP).

Also, when we pray for the leaders of our nation, we should pray for righteous advisors to surround them. Why is that so important? Because **take away the wicked from before the king, and his throne will be established in righteousness (moral and spiritual rectitude in every area and relation)** (Proverbs 25:5, AMP).

When our leaders are established in righteousness, we live quiet, peaceable lives in a land where the gospel is free to go forth. **I exhort therefore, that, first of all, supplications, prayers, intercessions, and giving of thanks, be made for all men; for kings, and for all that are in authority; that we may lead a quiet and peaceable life in all godliness and honesty. For this is good and acceptable in the sight of God our Saviour.** (1 Timothy 2:1-3).

Dwelling Securely in a World of Insecurity

Proverbs 28 includes many axioms that describe the person who perverts justice. Then a promise is given to all the upright in heart who guard the ways of justice before God: *He who walks uprightly shall be safe*, **but he who willfully goes in double and wrong ways shall fall in one of them** (v. 18, AMP).

You know, we live in a time of insecurity. Crime and injustice are on the increase in almost every realm of life.

That point was driven home to me one night as I rode my bicycle around the neighborhood. I passed a lovely new house that had just been built, when suddenly I noticed something that struck me: The house had bars on the door!

That's the kind of insecure world we live in today. People feel they have to put bars on their windows and doors for security.

But as believers, our security isn't in natural things. It doesn't hurt for us to secure our home the best we can, but our confidence and trust have to be in the Lord. And I'll tell you why — because natural man hasn't invented anything that can protect us fully, with or without bars on the windows and doors.

If you have been going to bed afraid at night, start trusting in the Lord for your safety and security. Remember the promise you can hold on to as you walk in God's wisdom: **Whoso hearkens to me [Wisdom] shall dwell securely and in confident trust and shall be quiet, without fear or dread of evil** (Proverbs 1:33, AMP).

Keep Psalm 91 in your heart. Read it morning and night if you are plagued by fear.

For God hath not given us the spirit of fear; but of power, and of love, and of a sound mind (2 Timothy 1:7).

Fear is a spirit. Rebuke it in the name of Jesus anytime it speaks to you.

You don't have to be afraid. God gives you His promise of security: **My people shall dwell in a peaceable habitation, in safe dwellings, and in quiet resting-places** (Isaiah 32:18, AMP).

That's a wonderful promise to stand on! I say things like that over my home all the time: "My home is a safe dwelling and a quiet resting place, because the power of God secures my life, my loved ones and my belongings." Make this the confession of *your* mouth. Guard the ways of justice by praying for your nation's leaders and showing kindness to the poor.

As you walk in God's ways and do what is right in His sight, you have His promise that you *will* be safe. The Lord is your Refuge, and He causes you to dwell securely in the land in all **quietness and confident trust forever** (Isaiah 32:17, AMP).

Wisdom for Today

❧

Be kind and give to the poor.

Guard the ways of justice by praying for your nation's leaders.

Rebuke fear the moment it speaks to you, and confess daily,
"My home is a safe dwelling and a quiet resting place because
the power of God secures my life, my loved ones and my belongings."

CHAPTER 29
The Danger of a Hard Heart

*If we are to walk in God's wisdom and find His perfect
will for our lives, we must heed His urgent warning:
"Today if you hear My voice, do not harden your heart."*

❦

Proverbs Chapter 29

1 He, that being often reproved hardeneth his neck, shall suddenly be destroyed, and that without remedy.

2 When the righteous are in authority, the people rejoice: but when the wicked beareth rule, the people mourn.

3 Whoso loveth wisdom rejoiceth his father: but he that keepeth company with harlots spendeth his substance.

4 The king by judgment establisheth the land: but he that receiveth gifts overthroweth it.

5 A man that flattereth his neighbour spreadeth a net for his feet.

6 In the transgression of an evil man there is a snare: but the righteous doth sing and rejoice.

7 The righteous considereth the cause of the poor: but the wicked regardeth not to know it.

8 Scornful men bring a city into a snare: but wise men turn away wrath.

9 If a wise man contendeth with a foolish man, whether he rage or laugh, there is no rest.

10 The bloodthirsty hate the upright: but the just seek his soul.

11 A fool uttereth all his mind: but a wise man keepeth it in till afterwards.

12 If a ruler hearken to lies, all his servants are wicked.

13 The poor and the deceitful man meet together: the Lord lighteneth both their eyes.

14 The king that faithfully judgeth the poor, his throne shall be established for ever.

15 The rod and reproof give wisdom: but a child left to himself bringeth his mother to shame.

16 When the wicked are multiplied, transgression increaseth: but the righteous shall see their fall.

17 Correct thy son, and he shall give thee rest; yea, he shall give delight unto thy soul.

18 Where there is no vision, the people perish: but he that keepeth the law, happy is he.

19 A servant will not be corrected by words: for though he understand he will not answer.

20 Seest thou a man that is hasty in his words? there is more hope of a fool than of him.

21 He that delicately bringeth up his servant from a child shall have him become his son at the length.

22 An angry man stirreth up strife, and a furious man aboundeth in transgression.

23 A man's pride shall bring him low: but honour shall uphold the humble in spirit.

24 Whoso is partner with a thief hateth his own soul: he heareth cursing, and bewrayeth it not.

25 The fear of man bringeth a snare: but whoso putteth his trust in the Lord shall be safe.

26 Many seek the ruler's favour; but every man's judgment cometh from the Lord.

27 An unjust man is an abomination to the just: and he that is upright in the way is abomination to the wicked.

Hidden Treasures

I want to cover a very important principle in Proverbs 29, and it's found in the very first verse: **He who, being often reproved, hardens his neck shall suddenly be destroyed — and that without remedy** (v. 1, AMP). It's such a dangerous risk to allow one's heart to become hardened that it's worth taking some time to focus our attention on the subject.

The Lie of "Maybe Later"

Some people who have repeatedly heard the gospel falsely believe they can just keep putting off a commitment to Jesus Christ until later. They think, *Well, I know the kind of lifestyle I'm living isn't right. But I'll just live this way a while longer. When I'm older, then I'll make a change.*

Their attitude is, *I know what's right, but I want to keep doing what's wrong.* However, there is a big problem with thinking that way. A person's heart becomes more and more hardened every time the Spirit of God deals with him and he says no. His heart can finally become so hardened that he will be left to eat the fruit of his own way (Proverbs 1:31).

Even when the Holy Spirit continues to deal with that person, he can reach the place where sin is so commonplace and accepted in his life, he refuses to be corrected or brought to repentance. (It isn't that God will not forgive him if he repents. If he will turn to the Lord even with his dying breath, God will receive him.)

That's the kind of situation Proverbs 29:1 is talking about. The person who is often reproved hardens his neck.

You are taking a terrible chance when you continue doing what you know isn't right. In the first place, you can cut your life short because sin opens the door to the devil. Secondly, you can't predict what kind of toll sin will take on your life in the meantime. You can fool around and resist the Holy Spirit until you completely harden your heart to Him.

Don't be deceived into thinking, *I'll live in sin for a while and then change later.* That's the devil's lie! You don't know for sure if you'll be able to bring yourself to change later on down the road. You could become so hardened you wouldn't want to repent, even though God is always ready to forgive you.

Another problem with thinking that way is, it may be "later" than you think. Today may be the last day you have on earth unless you put yourself in God's hands under His protection. The Scripture says TODAY!

Israel's Provocation in the Wilderness

I'll tell you, sin is a deadly thing. It will ruin your life. That's why God strongly warns us, **To day if ye will hear his voice, Harden not your hearts, as in the provocation, in the day of temptation in the wilderness** (Hebrews 3:7-8).

At times the Spirit of God will correct you or tell you what you need to do. He'll warn you in your spirit, "This isn't right. It's against the Word of God." If you don't respond to that inward leading, you're resisting both the Word and the Holy Spirit. That's how your heart grows callous toward God.

That's what happened to the children of Israel in the wilderness. They hardened their hearts to God's instruction.

The Israelites witnessed many miracles as God delivered them from the bondage of Egypt. God wanted to bring them into the Promised Land, a land where there was abundance of everything. God wanted them to dispossess the heathen by laying up His Word in their hearts and obeying it, so that their days could be multiplied and they could live in days of heaven upon the earth (Deuteronomy 11:18-28).

However, when God told the Israelites to go up against their enemies and take the land, they refused to do it. They wouldn't grasp hold of God's instruction and mix it with faith (Hebrews 4:2).

So the ten spies returned from the land with a bad report. They declared, "Those who dwell in the land are too big for us!" and the Israelites believed them. Yet the other two spies, Joshua and Caleb, declared, "We *can* take the land. God is with us!" But the people chose to harden their hearts and agree with the report of doubt and unbelief (Numbers 13-14).

This wasn't the first time the people had agreed with the enemy. Again and again God had reproved them for their disobedience and unbelief, and again and again they had hardened their hearts and not listened.

But this was one time too many for God. The people had pushed God too far. He said, "That's it! You've tested and tried Me these ten times. You are not ever going to see the land, only more wilderness" (Numbers 14:22-23, author's paraphrase). The wisdom in Proverbs 29:1 came to pass in their lives — their own hard hearts had broken them without remedy.

That wasn't God's will. It was His will that the Israelites possess the land. But they wouldn't do it God's way, so He sent them back into the wilderness to die. All those who hardened their necks against God lost their opportunity to enter the Promised Land.

And here's what's ironic! When God told the people to go back to the wilderness, they rebelled again and said, "No, now we want to fight!"

Moses told them, "Don't go up; the Lord is not with you. You'll be defeated!" But once again, they hardened their hearts against God's counsel and went up to try to conquer the Canaanites and Amalekites. The Israelites suffered a great defeat, just as God said they would (Numbers 14:40-45).

Over the next forty years, everyone more than twenty years old died in the wilderness, except Joshua and Caleb. These two men of faith received God's Word and were willing to obey it. God kept them strong and alive.

When Caleb was eighty years old, he came out of that wilderness just as strong as when he went into it. He was still believing God, still strong in body, declaring, "God, give me that mountain. If the Lord be with me, then I shall be able to drive them out!" (Joshua 14:6-13).

But all the others who had hardened their hearts died. God said, **They do alway err in their heart; and they have not known my ways. So I sware in my wrath, They shall not enter into my rest** (Hebrews 3:10-11).

Mix God's Word With Faith

The children of Israel couldn't enter the Promised Land because of their unbelief, so God had to raise up a new generation to take the land.

You see, the sin of unbelief gives the devil a foothold that keeps you from receiving God's promise in your life. The Word must be mixed with faith if is to be effective in your life (Hebrews 4:2). The promise of God has to be heard and believed.

I could teach the Word to you all day long, but if you don't mix it with faith and apply it to your own life, the Word won't profit you at all. In fact, you could come away from hearing the Word worse off than you were before! How? By hardening your heart against the truth and saying, "I've tried that, and it doesn't work. It's too good to be true."

We don't want to follow the Israelites' example. When God reproves and corrects us, we must listen and immediately obey. If we want to prosper and be blessed, we have to follow God.

Sin's Deceitfulness
Hardens Hearts

The final end of a hardened heart doesn't just happen overnight. Sometimes it takes years of sowing stout words and disobedience against God to bring calamity into your life.

In praying for people who are in a coma, I've found that the outcome of the situation — whether or not my faith can help bring them out of the coma — depends on the seeds they've sown in their lives. It depends on the words *they've* spoken and the divine instructions they have obeyed or disobeyed.

Sometimes people have just pushed God too far out of their lives. And seeds of disobedience have set spiritual laws into motion that someone else cannot reverse.

I'm telling you, it is a serious thing to harden our hearts and stiffen our necks against God. God's warning is stern: **Take heed, brethren, lest there be in any of you an evil heart of unbelief, in departing from the living God. But exhort one another daily, while it is called To day; lest any of you be hardened through the deceitfulness of sin** (Hebrews 3:12-13).

We need to be exhorted daily from the Word so our minds will continue to think according to God's wisdom. Without the wisdom of God, our hearts can be so hardened that sin becomes acceptable to us.

The world wants you to think that sin is the norm. And when you play around with sin, it's easy to start thinking that way. You can become hardened by its deceitfulness.

God may be dealing with you about an area of your life that isn't right. You need to repent and change some things, and you know it.

Well, don't just assume that you have forever to decide or that He will continue to deal with you indefinitely. And don't think the sin will become easier to deal with in time. It won't get any easier; in fact, it will get harder as time goes on.

So don't put God off. He is trying to help you because He loves you. Don't harden your heart to His loving reproof. Accept it, obey it and move on in your walk with Him to do whatever He's calling you to do!

Wisdom for Today

When the Holy Spirit warns you in your spirit, "What you're doing isn't right," obey that inward leading to change.

Follow Caleb's example. When God tells you to do something, let your attitude be, "Lord, give me that mountain. I can possess it!"

Mix the Word with faith so it can be effective in your life.

CHAPTER 30
Give Honor to Your Parents

Do you want long life and good days on this earth?
Then follow two of God's most basic commands: Honor
your parents, and walk in love.

๙(๏)๛

Proverbs Chapter 30

1   The words of Agur the son of Jakeh, even the prophecy: the man spake unto Ithiel, even unto Ithiel and Ucal,

2   Surely I am more brutish than any man, and have not the understanding of a man.

3   I neither learned wisdom, nor have the knowledge of the holy.

4   Who hath ascended up into heaven, or descended? who hath gathered the wind in his fists? who hath bound the waters in a garment? who hath established all the ends of the earth? what is his name, and what is his son's name, if thou canst tell?

5   Every word of God is pure: he is a shield unto them that put their trust in him.

6   Add thou not unto his words, lest he reprove thee, and thou be found a liar.

7   Two things have I required of thee; deny me them not before I die:

8   Remove far from me vanity and lies: give me neither poverty nor riches; feed me with food convenient for me:

9   Lest I be full, and deny thee, and say, Who is the Lord? or lest I be poor, and steal, and take the name of my God in vain.

10   Accuse not a servant unto his master, lest he curse thee, and thou be found guilty.

11   There is a generation that curseth their father, and doth not bless their mother.

12   There is a generation that are pure in their own eyes, and yet is not washed from their filthiness.

13   There is a generation, O how lofty are their eyes! and their eyelids are lifted up.

14   There is a generation, whose teeth are as swords, and their jaw teeth as knives, to devour the poor from off the earth, and the needy from among men.

15   The horseleach hath two daughters, crying, Give, give. There are three things that are never satisfied, yea, four things say not, It is enough:

16   The grave; and the barren womb; the earth that is not filled with water; and the fire that saith not, It is enough.

17   The eye that mocketh at his father, and despiseth to obey his mother, the ravens of the valley shall pick it out, and the young eagles shall eat it.

18   There be three things which are too wonderful for me, yea, four which I know not:

19   The way of an eagle in the air; the way of a serpent upon a rock; the way of a ship in the midst of the sea; and the way of a man with a maid.

20 Such is the way of an adulterous woman; she eateth, and wipeth her mouth, and saith, I have done no wickedness.

21 For three things the earth is disquieted, and for four which it cannot bear:

22 For a servant when he reigneth; and a fool when he is filled with meat;

23 For an odious woman when she is married; and an handmaid that is heir to her mistress.

24 There be four things which are little upon the earth, but they are exceeding wise:

25 The ants are a people not strong, yet they prepare their meat in the summer;

26 The conies are but a feeble folk, yet make they their houses in the rocks;

27 The locusts have no king, yet go they forth all of them by bands;

28 The spider taketh hold with her hands, and is in kings' palaces.

29 There be three things which go well, yea, four are comely in going:

30 A lion which is strongest among beasts, and turneth not away for any;

31 A greyhound; an he goat also; and a king, against whom there is no rising up.

32 If thou hast done foolishly in lifting up thyself, or if thou hast thought evil, lay thine hand upon thy mouth.

33 Surely the churning of milk bringeth forth butter, and the wringing of the nose bringeth forth blood: so the forcing of wrath bringeth forth strife.

Hidden Treasures

Honoring one's parents is very important to God. We're going to look at God's promised blessings to those who honor their parents. But first let's look at Proverbs 30, where God warns of the danger of *dishonoring* one's father and mother.

The First Commandment
With a Promise

God can be quite graphic when He wants to get a point across. Look at His description of the person who dishonors his parents: **The eye that mocks a father and scorns to obey a mother, the ravens of the valley will pick it out, and the young vultures will devour it** (Proverbs 30:17, AMP).

In other words, God is letting us know that it definitely won't go well with us if we don't honor our parents!

On the other hand, God promises great blessings to those who honor their parents: **Children, obey your parents in the Lord [as His representatives], for this is just and right. Honor (esteem and value as precious) your father and your mother — this is the first commandment with a promise — That all may be well with you and that you may live long on the earth** (Ephesians 6:1-3, AMP).

You see, God's promise goes with the commandment to honor your parents. If you honor, esteem and value them as precious, things will go well with you in this life. Not only that, but God promises you will live long on this earth.

Obey Parents in the Lord

Notice God's command to children is, **Obey your parents *in the Lord*.** That is speaking of parents who are following God and not parents who are acting contrary to God's Word.

Of course, Ephesians was written to Christians, not to the world. For the most part, children in Christian families won't face the kind of difficult situations some children in the world go through.

Overcoming Strife With God's Love

Many Christian families do face problems, however, between parents and children. In some Christian homes, the father and mother love and honor God, but the children have gone astray and are dishonoring their parents in the process. These children can just count on it: Things will *not* go well with them.

In other Christian families, the parents aren't fulfilling their responsibility to raise their children **[tenderly] in the training and discipline and the counsel and admonition of the Lord** (Ephesians 6:4, AMP).

The missing ingredient in both these situations is the love of God.

God's Love Makes a Family Work

You see, God's love is the spiritual force that makes a family enjoy life together. Being a member of a family that loves God and one another is the most wonderful blessing. If strife exists in a Christian home between children and their parents, what should a family do? First of all, every parent needs to make the quality decision, *I'm going to walk in love with my children. I won't be overbearing, nor irritate or provoke my children to anger* (Ephesians 6:4, AMP).

Each child also needs to make a quality decision. They should receive God's Word about honoring their parents and settle it in their heart: *From now on, I'm going to obey and honor my parents.*

The love of God is the one force that will overcome every strife-filled situation, every age barrier and every generation gap. God's love is what helps a family to work together as a strong unit.

Our family is a strong unit knit together by love. Our children love us; we love them; and they love one another. We're not in strife with one another. We support each other, pray for each other and help each other.

That's the way it should be in every family — the love of God continually manifested in our midst. When acted upon, love will overcome all failures and resistance.

Learning to walk in love has to start somewhere. Parents ought to forbear their children, rearing them tenderly in the admonition of the Lord — always in the love of God. Children ought to forbear their parents, obeying them and showing them honor. And neither parents *nor* children should wait for the other side to start doing their part first!

Don't be placed in the **class of people who curse their fathers and do not bless their mothers** (Proverbs 30:11, AMP). Be counted with those who obey God's command to honor their mother and father. Then you can boldly claim God's promise: "Thank You, Father, that all will go well with me as I live long on this earth!"

Wisdom for Today

꽃✑✑

Honor your parents, esteeming them and valuing them as precious.

Make the quality decision, "I'm going to walk in love with my children. I won't irritate or provoke them to anger."

Let the love of God rule in your home — and let it start with you!

CHAPTER 31
The Virtuous Woman —
The Glorious Church

The picture of the virtuous woman in Proverbs 31
stands as an example of the holiness and virtue we
must walk in to prepare for Jesus' soon return. He is
coming sooner than we think for His family!

Proverbs Chapter 31

1   The words of king Lemuel, the prophecy that his mother taught him.

2   What, my son? and what, the son of my womb? and what, the son of my vows?

3   Give not thy strength unto women, nor thy ways to that which destroyeth kings.

4   It is not for kings, O Lemuel, it is not for kings to drink wine; nor for princes strong drink:

5   Lest they drink, and forget the law, and pervert the judgment of any of the afflicted.

6   Give strong drink unto him that is ready to perish, and wine unto those that be of heavy hearts.

7   Let him drink, and forget his poverty, and remember his misery no more.

8   Open thy mouth for the dumb in the cause of all such as are appointed to destruction.

9   Open thy mouth, judge righteously, and plead the cause of the poor and needy.

10   Who can find a virtuous woman? for her price is far above rubies.

11   The heart of her husband doth safely trust in her, so that he shall have no need of spoil.

12   She will do him good and not evil all the days of her life.

13   She seeketh wool, and flax, and worketh willingly with her hands.

14   She is like the merchants' ships; she bringeth her food from afar.

15   She riseth also while it is yet night, and giveth meat to her household, and a portion to her maidens.

16   She considereth a field, and buyeth it: with the fruit of her hands she planteth a vineyard.

17   She girdeth her loins with strength, and strengtheneth her arms.

18   She perceiveth that her merchandise is good: her candle goeth not out by night.

19   She layeth her hands to the spindle, and her hands hold the distaff.

20   She stretcheth out her hand to the poor; yea, she reacheth forth her hands to the needy.

21   She is not afraid of the snow for her household: for all her household are clothed with scarlet.

22   She maketh herself coverings of tapestry; her clothing is silk and purple.

23 Her husband is known in the gates, when he sitteth among the elders of the land.

24 She maketh fine linen, and selleth it; and delivereth girdles unto the merchant.

25 Strength and honour are her clothing; and she shall rejoice in time to come.

26 She openeth her mouth with wisdom; and in her tongue is the law of kindness.

27 She looketh well to the ways of her household, and eateth not the bread of idleness.

28 Her children arise up, and call her blessed; her husband also, and he praiseth her.

29 Many daughters have done virtuously, but thou excellest them all.

30 Favour is deceitful, and beauty is vain: but a woman that feareth the Lord, she shall be praised.

31 Give her of the fruit of her hands; and let her own works praise her in the gates.

Hidden Treasures

Proverbs 31 holds up before us a wonderful picture of a virtuous woman. Among other desirable qualities, she is a woman of faithfulness, diligence, kindness, generosity and strength.

The dictionary defines "virtue" as *moral excellence; right action and thinking; goodness.* That sounds a lot like holiness, doesn't it? That's what we're going to talk about in this final chapter of Proverbs: the call to holiness coming from the very throne of God. Jesus is making ready His Church.

The Last Great Frontier

Today the Church is standing at the edge of a great frontier. I believe it is the final frontier that stands between us and the fullness of God's glory. On the other side lie the greatest manifestations of God's power this earth has ever seen.

What is this last, great spiritual frontier? *Holiness.* And we will cross it before Jesus comes to catch us away. I know we will because the Bible says He is coming for a glorious Church without spot or wrinkle (Ephesians 5:27). In other words, Jesus is coming for a Church that is holy.

The word "holiness" simply means *separation to God or conduct befitting those so separated.* "To separate" means *to set apart; to disunite; to disconnect; to go a different direction.*

If we want to be holy, we must disconnect ourselves from the world and its ways and become connected to God and His ways.

"But we're just human," you may say. "Is it really possible for us to be holy?"

Yes, it is because we've been born of God. Our new spirit is made in His image. We were separated to God when we made Jesus our Lord and Savior. He has put Himself in us by His Spirit.

As we yield to and are taught and guided by His Spirit, our spiritual birth and separation to God are manifested in the natural part of our makeup. We begin to act and talk like God lives in us. We walk in Him and He walks in us (2 Corinthians 6:16).

Led Into Holiness

Holiness is not a special calling that only a few people have. Holiness is a quality in which every person in the Body of Christ is called. **For God hath not called us unto uncleanness, but unto holiness** (1 Thessalonians 4:7). We've been given the robe of righteousness, but we must maintain it.

The Holy Spirit lives inside us just for that purpose — to direct us in holiness and wisdom. And we do our part by choosing to hearken to and obey Him (Hebrews 8:10-12).

When you fellowship with God and stay in living, vital contact with Him, the Holy Spirit will lead you into holiness. For example, He will say to you, "Don't use profane language. You don't need that. Use words that glorify the Lord." Or He'll say, "You don't have time for those worldly novels. Read more of the Word."

You don't have to change in your own strength. Whatever the Holy Spirit asks you to do, He also empowers you to do. The Bible says that He gives us the strength to overcome every temptation (1 Corinthians 10:13). God is not being dictatorial. He just wants you to be free.

No Excuse for Unholiness

That's why the New Testament speaks to us so strongly about holiness. Nowhere does God say, "Well, I know you Christians have sinned a lot lately, but, hey, I understand. Life is tough, and at least you're trying."

No! He just says, **Be ye holy, for I am holy** (1 Peter 1:16).

We have no excuse for living unholy lives. God not only prompts us to be holy — He enables us to do it!

I'm telling you, it's high time we took advantage of the power of God's Holy Spirit who indwells us. We've reached the end of the age. Jesus is coming sooner than we think for His Church. It is time to get the slack out of our lives and become absolutely focused on God. It's time we drop everything that pulls us away from Him. It's time to get our flesh under control and yield only to the Holy Spirit.

We ought not look like the world and talk and act like the world. We ought to look and talk and act like God! The Bible says, **As the One Who called you is holy, you yourselves also be holy in all your conduct and manner of living** (1 Peter 1:15, AMP).

The Glorious Church Is
The Holy Church

Some people get more excited about being the glorious Church than they do about being the holy Church. They have the idea that the glory of God is exciting, but holiness is boring. But that's not true! Glory and holiness are both wonderful qualities — and you can't have the fullness of one without the other.

The reason is simple. Holiness is what allows the glory of God to be manifested. So the more we walk in holiness and virtue, the more God can pour forth Himself through us! Glory is God Himself, being seen and felt or revealed to our natural senses. God has said the righteous will shine with the glory of God. Jesus is sanctifying His Church and cleansing it by the washing of water by the Word so **that he might present it to himself a glorious church, not having spot, or wrinkle, or any such thing; but that it should be holy and without blemish** (Ephesians 5:27).

Now, you might say, "But I don't know if I can be holy, without spot or blemish." God doesn't expect us to be able to grow up without making mistakes. Thank God for the blood of Jesus. That precious blood is always available to cleanse us from sin so that "all of our household can be clothed in scarlet" (Proverbs 31:21). **But if we walk in the light, as he is in the light, we have fellowship one with another, and the blood of Jesus Christ his Son cleanseth us from all sin.... If we confess our sins, he is faithful and just to**

forgive us our sins, and to cleanse us from all unrighteousness (1 John 1:7,9).

When you miss the mark (that's what sin means), let Jesus cleanse you and keep pressing toward the mark of the high calling of God, forgetting those things that are behind and stretching forth unto those marvelous things that lie just ahead (Philippians 3:13-14).

Set your sights on being holy as Jesus is holy, and seek after the wisdom of God with all your heart. Let the picture of the virtuous woman of Proverbs 31 stand as an example of the holiness and virtue you are called to walk in as you prepare for Jesus' soon return.

By the grace of God, Jesus is coming for a glorious Church. No one else can fulfill our role on this earth as the Body of Christ. We're it! We're all God has. And because He is God, He can bring forth His holiness in us!

Wisdom for Today

Disconnect yourself from the world and its ways and connect yourself to God and His ways.

Stay in living contact with the Holy Spirit so He can lead you into holiness and into His purpose in your life.

Get the slack out of your life and become absolutely focused on God! Expect His Glory to be revealed in you and to you.

About the Author

Gloria Copeland is a noted author and minister of the gospel whose teaching ministry is known throughout the world. Believers worldwide know her through Believers' Conventions, Victory Campaigns, magazine articles, teaching tapes and videos, and the daily and Sunday *Believer's Voice of Victory* television broadcast, which she hosts with her husband, Kenneth Copeland. She is known for "Healing School," which she began teaching and hosting in 1979 at KCM meetings. Gloria delivers the Word of God and the keys to victorious Christian living to millions of people every year.

Gloria has written many books, including *God's Will for You, Walk With God, God's Will Is Prosperity, Walk in the Spirit* and *Living Contact.* She has also co-authored several books with her husband, including *Family Promises, Healing Promises* and the best-selling daily devotional, *From Faith to Faith.*

She holds an honorary doctorate from Oral Roberts University. In 1994, Gloria was voted Christian Woman of the Year, an honor conferred on women whose example demonstrates outstanding Christian leadership. Gloria is also the co-founder and vice president of Kenneth Copeland Ministries in Fort Worth, Texas.

Learn more about Kenneth Copeland Ministries by visiting our website at www.kcm.org.

Books by Gloria Copeland

And Jesus Healed Them All
Are You Ready?
Build Your Financial Foundation
Build Yourself an Ark
Fight On!
God's Prescription for Divine Health
God's Success Formula
God's Will for You
God's Will for Your Healing
God's Will Is Prosperity
**God's Will Is the Holy Spirit*
**Harvest of Health*
Living Contact
**Love — The Secret to Your Success*
No Deposit — No Return
Pleasing the Father
Pressing In — It's Worth It All
The Power to Live a New Life
The Unbeatable Spirit of Faith
**Walk in the Spirit*
Walk With God
Well Worth the Wait

*Available in Spanish

Books Co-Authored by Kenneth and Gloria Copeland

Family Promises
Healing Promises
Prosperity Promises
From Faith to Faith — A Daily Guide to Victory

World Offices
of Kenneth Copeland Ministries

For more information about KCM and a free
catalog, please write the office nearest you:

Kenneth Copeland Ministries
Fort Worth, Texas 76192-0001

Kenneth Copeland
Locked Bag 2600
Mansfield Delivery Centre
QUEENSLAND 4122
AUSTRALIA

Kenneth Copeland
Private Bag X 909
FOUNTAINEBLEAU
2032
REPUBLIC OF SOUTH AFRICA

Kenneth Copeland
Post Office Box 15
BATH
BA1 1GD
ENGLAND

Kenneth Copeland
Post Office Box 378
Surrey
BRITISH COLUMBIA
V3T 5B6
CANADA

UKRAINE
L'VIV 290000
Post Office Box 84
Kenneth Copeland Ministries
L'VIV 290000
UKRAINE

Additional copies of this book
are available from your local bookstore
or from:

HARRISON HOUSE
P. O. Box 35035
Tulsa, Oklahoma 74153

The Harrison House Vision

Proclaiming the truth and the power
Of the Gospel of Jesus Christ
With excellence;
Challenging Christians to
Live victoriously,
Grow spiritually,
Know God intimately.

We're Here for You!

Believer's Voice of Victory Television Broadcast

Join Kenneth and Gloria Copeland, and the *Believer's Voice of Victory* broadcasts, Monday through Friday and on Sunday each week, and learn how God can change your life from ordinary to extraordinary. This is some of the best teaching you'll ever hear designed to get you where you want to be — *on top!*

You can catch the *Believer's Voice of Victory* broadcast on your local, cable or satellite channels.

*Check your local listing for times and stations in your area.

Believer's Voice of Victory Magazine

Enjoy inspired teaching and encouragement from Kenneth and Gloria Copeland each month in the *Believer's Voice of Victory* magazine. Also included are real-life testimonies of God's miraculous power and divine intervention into the lives of people just like you!

It's more than just a magazine — it's a ministry.

Shout! ...The dynamic magazine just for kids!

Shout! The Voice of Victory for Kids is a Bible-charged, action-packed, bimonthly magazine available FREE to kids everywhere! Featuring *Wichita Slim* and *Commander Kellie* and *the Superkids*SM, *Shout!* is filled with colorful adventure comics, challenging games and puzzles, exciting short stories, solve-it-yourself mysteries and much more!!

Stand up, sign up and get ready to *Shout!*

To receive a FREE subscription to *Believer's Voice of Victory*, or
to give a child you know a FREE subscription to *Shout!*, write or call:

Kenneth Copeland Ministries
Fort Worth, Texas 76192-0001

Or call:
1-800-359-0075
(9 a.m.-5 p.m. CT)